D1760022

Yorkshire Fishing Fleets

65p

Dalesman books of related interest:

ROBIN HOOD'S BAY

SHIPWRECKS OF THE YORKSHIRE COAST
(by Arthur Godfrey and Peter J. Lassey)

YORKSHIRE PORTS AND HARBOURS

Yorkshire Fishing Fleets

The story of Yorkshire's oldest
and most dangerous industry

by

Arthur Godfrey

Dalesman Books
1974

The Dalesman Publishing Company Ltd.,
Clapham (via Lancaster), North Yorkshire
First published 1974
© Arthur Godfrey 1974
ISBN: 0 85206 245 1

To all those who wrest a living from the North Sea, and to the fishermen of Yorkshire in particular.

Printed and Bound in Great Britain by
Ellesmere Press Ltd., Mill Lane, Skipton, North Yorkshire

Contents

The front cover photograph is of Whitby harbour.

Back cover illustrations:- Top: Paddle trawler *Spurn*, run down and sunk in 1898. Bottom: The ill-fated steam trawler *Crystal*, sunk by a mine off Scarborough in 1943.

Photographs in the text are on pages 33 - 36 and 53 - 56.

The maps and line drawings are by the author.

Introduction

IT is difficult to over-estimate the way in which the people of the British Isles have been affected by man's quest for food from the sea. Since time immemorial, man has been compelled to devote a great deal of his time and energy to the problems of finding food, and now, as the twenty-first century approaches, the problem grows still. Though we may sometimes congratulate ourselves on the ways in which technology has helped to meet our ever-increasing demand for food, it is a sobering thought to realise that fish, one of our staple food items, is still hunted in the wilds as it was in the stone-age. The equipment used to carry out the hunting is of course highly sophisticated today, but the principle remains the same as ever.

Perhaps it is the fact that they are the last true hunters that sets fishermen apart from the rest of us, and makes them the object of awe and admiration from ordinary "landlubbers". Hunting for food has always been a dangerous and difficult occupation, and remains so to this day. The fisherman's life has always been fraught with hazard; statistics provided in 1972 showed that the death-risk in fishing was 40 times greater than that in mining, and 100 times greater than that in manufacturing industries. These are staggering figures; the dangers in mining have always been only too clear, yet the dangers in fishing are in fact much greater. As one Scarborough fisherman was overheard to say in a harbourside pub recently, "There are no back doors at sea". Trawlermen are only too aware that if they are lost at sea, their dependents will receive a £2,000 death-benefit—as the fishermen cynically put it, the money is the "first prize", awarded to those who "go over the wall".

Fishing has always been big business since the end of the middle-ages, and disputes in the industry have involved kings, government and even the various churches at different times. The history of the British fishing industry is a story of violence, suffering and death; a constant struggle with the sea, the elements and human enemies. Wars have been waged over the right to fish, and fishermen have been executed for fishing in someone else's grounds. Thankfully, dangers of this kind have largely disappeared, but the battle with

7

the elements is not yet won, nor will it ever be. In 1974 one of our very best and most modern trawlers, the *Gaul*, disappeared with her crew of 36 men, and no trace has been found of her.

The men who man today's fishing craft are, perhaps for the first time, well paid for their labours, and many a shoreworker envies the fisherman's paypacket. The fish in the sea belong to no-one; there is nothing to stop anyone from buying a boat, and becoming a fisherman—if he can, and if he dare. In an attempt to ascertain properly the dangers of the fishing industry today, a ten-year survey into the casualty rate among Hull fishermen is currently being carried out, and the results of this are sure to make sombre reading.

This book is an attempt to outline the history of the fishing industry of the Yorkshire coast, and to indicate, by describing some of the many tragedies, what a painful past it has had.

1.   Early History

No-ONE can now be certain just how or when fishing in the North
Sea began, but there is evidence to show that it dates back to
Roman days, for fishing hooks from that period have been found
in river estuaries. The Vikings, who invaded Yorkshire's coast in
the ninth century, were known to be fishermen—in fact it has been
suggested that herring fishing may have been one reason for the
Viking invasion. There was a migration of herring to England's
eastern shores at this time, and the Vikings may have been following
the shoals when they came here. As early as 836 A.D., the Nether-
landers are said to have visited the north-east coast of Britain for
the purpose of buying saltfish, and herring almost certainly com-
prised part of this trade.

The Vikings must have taught their fishing skills to the Yorkshire
communities, for from this time on, fishing and the sale of fish
became the main source of the national wealth, after wool sales.
Herring became so important that they almost replaced money as
currency! According to the Domesday Book, the town of Sandwich
paid a rent of £50 and 40,000 herrings. Nearer home, the monasteries
collected tithes from Yorkshire fishermen—often in the form of
herring—and there were frequent disputes about whether the tithes
on fish caught at Filey should go to the Prior at Bridlington, or to
the Abbot of Whitby. Various settlements were made over the
years, but it was not until the year 1190 that the Abbot lost all his
claim to the Filey tithes.

Another indication of just how seriously fishing was taken is
given by the fact that boats from the east coast were regularly
visiting Iceland by the twelfth century. This was a staggering
enterprize when one considers that the boats they used were really
no more than large open rowing boats, with a mast and single sail.
Strangely enough, even in those far-off days, the Icelanders complained that the English were ruining their fishing!

About the year 1165, the Dutch began herring fishing in the
North Sea, and quickly put our own fishermen to shame, as will be
seen later. The Danes too enjoyed wealth as a result of their herring
fishery; one author said of them in 1205; "The Danes, being a
maritime people, and constantly in their vessels, had formerly used

only the manner and dress of sailors, but now imitated the manners, dress and armour of other nations, and were clothed in scarlet, purple and fine linen, for they abounded in riches, by means of the fishery . . . which attracted merchants from all countries to purchase the herrings bestowed on them by the bounty of providence. Nor were the Danes only enriched; they were also polished and enlightened in consequence of their prosperous fishery, for learning became much more common among them than before, and the sons of Principal people were generally sent to finish their education at the University of Paris, then the most celebrated seminary in Europe."

On the Yorkshire coast, the herring fishery was of great importance too, particularly at Hull, where Cistercian monks from the local monastery controlled the industry—and of course reaped the profits. In medieval times, fresh fish was a most expensive item, available to few people. Most fish was either saltfish or dried fish, and herring of course was one of the easiest types of fish to preserve and the most convenient to export. For some reason, however, the Dutch far excelled us in the herring fishery, so much so that by 1542 many English harbours were falling into decay, because they were so little used. East coast fishermen were getting into the habit of buying herring from the Dutch, rather than catch their own, and the Dutchmen were catching the fish on our doorstep! In 1603, Sir Walter Raleigh complained bitterly about this in a pamphlet that he had published on the subject. He said that the greatest amount of fish ever known in the world was on the English coast, yet the English people gained no benefit from them, while boats from the Low Countries were taking herring to the value of £1,700,000 annually (probably a gross exaggeration). The Dutchmen paid for the privilege of fishing in English waters, however; in 1635 they paid no less than £30,000 to King Charles for permission to fish here.

Despite this, the English share of the trade increased gradually, and various monarchs encouraged the fishing industry from time to time. Apart from the obvious financial rewards, fishermen provided the nation with a kind of unofficial Naval reserve, a body of seafaring men who could in time of war be called on to man fighting ships. During the reign of Elizabeth I, and even later than this, attempts were made to compel people to eat fish on Wednesdays, as well as on Fridays, and for the whole of Lent. Ostensibly, this was done for religious reasons, but it is probably more realistic to think that it was done because we were rotten farmers, and fish was a good substitute for meat!

It was because fresh fish could not be kept fresh, nor moved far, that every town on the Yorkshire coast developed its own fishing industry. Each town or village would catch enough fish for its own needs, and the surplus would be sent overland as far as possible.

Stories are still told of the women from Robin Hood's Bay who used to walk as far inland as Pickering to sell fish which they carried in baskets over the moors. This particular village was described in Henry VIII's day as a "poor fisher town of twenty boats".

The type of craft in use by the Yorkshire fishing villages was a direct descendant of the Viking ships of earlier years. Known as the coble (pronounced "cobble" in Yorkshire), this type of boat is still in common use today in Yorkshire ports, even though the design is probably 1,000 years old. An Elizabethan authority said of it, ". . . two men will easily carry it on land between them, yet are so

Lug-rigged coble

secure in them at sea that some in a storm have lived aboard three days . . . " Other writers have described the coble as ". . . boat and harbour in one .. . ." and "probably the most perfect form of open sailing boat for putting out to sea in rough weather of any yet invented (lifeboats alone excepted)."

Cobles were designed for use on open beaches where there was no harbour and they were used principally for inshore line-fishing and for crab and lobster fishing. For herring fishing a larger type of boat known as a "five-man boat" was used, in the early nineteenth century. They were sometimes called "Farms", but this is probably a result of the way that Yorkshiremen run words together —"farmanboat". Strangely perhaps, five-man boats actually had a crew of seven; the name arose because five men worked the boat and did the fishing. The two extra hands were the cook and the boy, who were paid a wage for their services. The boats were clinker-built vessels of about sixty tons, and sixty feet in length. They had three masts, fitted with lugsails, and carried one or two cobles on the deck. During the season they followed the herring shoals as they moved south, remaining away from their home port for weeks and weeks at a time.

In the year 1817, a Government report on the fishing industry of the Yorkshire coast stated that there were 28 of these boats owned on the North Yorkshire coast, and half of these belonged to Staithes —which had no harbour at this time. There were 400 fishermen working from Staithes, while Robin Hood's Bay had 130 men manning forty boats, most of them small cobles. Runswick was another important fishing centre at this time; the three villages between them owned 140 vessels, a number which Scarborough, Whitby, Sandsend, Skinningrove, Saltburn, Marske and Redcar together could only just equal.

Further south, the fishing centres included Filey, which owned about forty cobles, and Flamborough, which had twice this number at its height. At both these places cobles were launched from the beach, as they are today. Filey was always important for its herring fishing too, and in later days a great part of the herring fleet based at Scarborough was Filey manned and owned. One of Flamborough's most interesting features was that, almost without exception, the cobles owned there were in the late 1800s built by one man, a local boat-builder named Hopwood.

The major ports of the Yorkshire coast took little part in fishing until the 1830s, when trawl-fishing was introduced to the area and the industry boomed. Until this time, fishing methods and boats had changed little since the Viking era.

2.   Sailing Trawlers and Drifters

IT should be understood that trawling as we know it today did not come into general use until the mid-nineteenth century. Before that date, long lining was used for catching demersal fish (those that swim near the bottom, e.g. cod) and drift or gill-nets to catch Pelagic fish (surface swimmers, e.g. herring and mackerel). In certain parts of England, however, experiments had for many years been carried out which involved dragging a bag-shaped net over the sea bed, i.e. trawling. It is thought that Brightlingsea fishermen had tried this method as early as 1377, but various authorities have differing ideas about precisely where it began. Certainly, it is known that two of the earliest ports to make use of beam trawl-fishing were Brixham in Devon, and Barking on the Thames. For various reasons, but particularly because they could not always find a market for their catch locally, Brixham trawlers began to work further afield. By the 1830s, they were working in the North Sea, and many of them used Hull and Scarborough as bases. In 1843, a fleet of Brixham trawlers made a discovery which led to a boom in the Yorkshire fishing industry.

They had for some time been working the Dogger Bank, the offshore shoal that stretches almost the full length of the Yorkshire Coast, when bad weather drove them off. The trawl nets were left down, perhaps because they had no time to haul them, or perhaps because they wanted to continue fishing as soon as they got off the Bank. Whatever the reason, they were to be thankful for it, for when the nets were raised they made the richest haul of sole that any of them had ever seen. The catch was made in deep water just off the Dogger Bank, an area that was to become known as the Silver Pits.

This discovery caused more Devon men to settle in Hull and Scarborough; within seven years more than a thousand southern fishermen had moved to Hull alone. Among them was a Brixham man named Robert Hellyer, who was later to found the famous steam trawling company that bore his name. Local people, however, appear to have been slow to take their share of this new wealth, but once they did begin, the industry grew very rapidly. In 1854, for instance, there were only 30 Hull registered smacks sailing for the North Sea grounds, but by 1863 there were 270. This number

13

Herring lugger of 1800

continued to grow until 1880, when there were 420 Hull smacks, though from then on their numbers declined as steam trawling began. Scarborough at this time owned 230 fishing vessels.

The word "smack", incidentally, did not define any particular type of boat or rig. Early smacks were lug-rigged on one or more masts. Later on they were rigged as cutters or sloops (single masted, fore and aft rigged vessels). However, the boat that was finally perfected for sailing-trawling, known also as a smack, was ketch-rigged, and this type of boat was, at its best, superb. Smacks had to be tremendously strong to withstand the buffeting of the North Sea, and they had to be fast, in view of the perishable nature of the cargo. The fact that they were heavily built enabled them to carry a lot of sail in winds which would force a lighter boat to take her sails in. Hence in bad weather, they could outpace even the fastest racing yacht. It was often said that the ketch-rigged sailing trawler was the finest fore-and-aft rigged vessel in use in Europe.

During this period of expansion, a Barking smack owner named Hewitt brought in another innovation, equipping his trawlers with ice for preserving the catch. Naturally, this extended the time that

14

Ketch-rigged sailing trawler of 1880

trawlers could spend at sea, and thus helped the boom in fishing. It led to yet another industry—obtaining or producing ice. Much of it was shipped from Norway, but farmers in England, particularly in flat areas, began flooding their fields during winter in order to produce ice. They went to great trouble to prevent would-be skaters from damaging their produce, and began to regard ice as a crop! Yet another factor in the development of the trawling industry was the coming of railways; ports like Hull found that they were able to distribute their catch further, and more quickly.

In order to catch and land the fish more efficiently, the "fleeting system" was adopted during the summer months. Large numbers of smacks fished together, remaining at sea for periods of up to three months. Periodically a carrier, which was usually a fast cutter, would collect the fish from each trawler and land it, usually taking it to the nearest port, but sometimes direct to Billingsgate. When they were not "fleeting", smacks usually remained at sea for up to fourteen days, bringing their catch with them when they docked. When this happened, the catch was iced aboard the smack, but in earlier days it was kept alive in salt water "wells".

Life for the smacksmen was extremely tough, and very uncomfortable. They had to take their sleep when they could, rarely more than four hours at a time, and often worked twenty-hour shifts. It was a non-stop cycle of shooting and hauling the nets, gutting then packing the fish, and repairing the gear, often right through the night.

Despite the fact that smacks were extremely seaworthy for their size—up to sixty feet long usually—there were times when the North Sea proved to be too much for them. Mariners have often

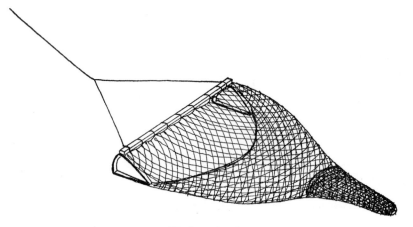

The beam trawl

said that the North Sea, despite its comparatively small size, can be as dangerous as any stretch of water in the world. What makes it particularly bad is the fact that foul weather can blow up with very little warning, certainly not enough to give a smack time to reach port. There were, of course, no weather forecasts via the radio to help them; only the sky and the seaman's instinct would indicate imminent storms. The Dogger Bank lies some forty miles or so from the Yorkshire coast ports, and this meant at least a four-hour trip to safety, assuming that the wind was favourable.

On 3 December 1863, a severe gale caused the loss of 24 smacks in the North Sea, and all the crews were drowned. Altogether, 144 men and boys died, but few of these were Yorkshiremen. Seven Hull men were among those lost, and one man died at Filey when the coble he was in capsized near the beach. Most of the damage was felt by Yarmouth boats, and despite the size of the tragedy, the *Scarborough Gazette* of this date says little about the incident, mainly because no Scarborough boats were involved in this particular storm. Added to this is the fact that by the time the next weekly edition of the paper came out, the news was already widely known by the fishing community.

Six years later, however, on 27 October 1869 Scarborough and Filey suffered a severe blow when the whole of their fleets were caught by a particularly ferocious storm. (Scarborough and Filey boats are grouped together because they all used the harbour at Scarborough, and all were registered at that port). There were in fact almost ninety vessels from Scarborough at sea, some of them having been out for fifteen days or more when the storm broke. The townspeople could do nothing but watch and wait, knowing that almost certainly some of their fishermen would not be returning.

On the morning of Thursday, 28 October, the smack *Achilles* arrived safely at Scarborough, though she had suffered a great deal of damage, and had lost most of her fishing gear. One by one, other local smacks limped into port, almost every one damaged, and all having lost their nets. Eventually it was reported that all of the 34 Filey owned boats were safe. However, three of the Scarborough fleet were missing, the *Rambler*, the *Prosperity* and the *John Wesley*.

The *Rambler*, an eight-year old vessel owned by James Sellers, had sailed on 12 October, commanded by John Gorbell. Altogether there were ten men aboard, including John Frazer, described as "a young man of colour", and another known locally as "Sunderland John". All ten died in the storm. The *Prosperity*, an eleven-year old vessel owned by a Mrs. Marshall and Messrs. T. Shaw and C. Clark, had sailed with the *Rambler*. There were eleven men aboard her, the extra hand being Mrs. Marshall's son, who was making his first voyage on a fishing boat. It proved also to be his last, for the *Prosperity* too was lost with all hands. Mrs. Marshall was thus deprived not only of a son, but also of her sole means of subsistence. The *John Wesley*, third of this ill-fated trio, was a yawl and not a smack—though the rig is only slightly different, yawls were used for drifting and not trawling. Eleven men were lost when the *John Wesley* sank, three of them Scarborough men, the remainder from Boston in Lincolnshire. Master of the yawl was one William Harwood, whose death was only a part of a staggering series of tragedies in his family—his father and son drowned with him, his mother died at their home during the voyage, and his sister was found to be dying of an incurable disease.

This series of disasters to the Scarborough fleet provoked a public meeting at the Town Hall, at which John Woodall, one-time Mayor of Scarborough, reported that the loss sustained by Scarborough and Filey amounted to some £20,000. The financial loss was not, however, the most serious result of the disaster. To quote from Mr. Woodall's report, as printed in the *Scarborough Gazette*. "Of course the larger portion of these losses fell upon those who might be called well-to-do and with whom they could but express their sympathy for the misfortune. They must, however, look to that class who, by the losses in question, had been deprived of their means of subsistence and who had no prospect but the workhouse before them, unless aided by the charitable and humane."

There were in fact some twelve widows and twenty-seven orphans left as a result of this disaster. Mr. Sellers, a local smack owner, reported that no less than 860 people had been "thrown out of employ" as a result of the storm. At this time, a smack was valued at between £400 and £600, and each carried nets and gear valued at approximately £450.

The smack *Achilles* was again involved in a fierce gale in 1880, and again she returned to port in safety to tell the anxious crowds of what had occurred. The *Achilles*, owned by George Levitt and skippered by Daniel Wright, had sailed on Monday, 25 October 1880. For two days the weather was beautiful, but by Wednesday night ominous storm clouds had begun to appear. The *Achilles* headed south, and when she was some 35 miles south-east of the Dogger Bank on Thursday night a gale was blowing and she found herself amidst great rolling seas. The smack had a good catch of fish aboard by this time, so headed for home. On Tuesday morning she arrived at Scarborough with her mainsail split, and her topmast carried away by the storm. On arrival, the crew found that the other smacks in the harbour were flying flags at half-mast, because three Scarborough skippers had been lost overboard during the gale. John Race and Robert Robson had been lost early in the storm, and James Pardon had met a similar fate the following day.

Pardon and a deckhand called Thomas Smith had been taking in the bowsprit on their yawl *Decision* when a big sea struck the vessel, throwing both men overboard. Smith managed to hang onto the vessel, and was hauled aboard, but Pardon was not seen again. One by one the fleet returned to port, all of them damaged, and many without their fishing gear. Eventually it was possible to count the cost, and it was found that four smacks had been totally lost in the storm.

The most serious of these losses was that of the *General Lee*, owned by William Purcell. She left Grimsby, from where she had been engaged in herring fishing, and was lost at sea with her crew of ten, mostly Filey or Bridlington men. The other smacks, the *Admiral Hope*, the *Gauntlet* and the *Spray*, were all driven ashore and wrecked near Bridlington, without loss of life. A fifth vessel, the Filey yawl *George Peabody*, was also stranded at Bridlington, but she was successfully refloated, and continued fishing until she was lost off Scarborough in 1888. This storm of October 1880 claimed dozens of vessels all along the Yorkshire coast; the fishing boat losses made up only a very small part of the total.

The chances of being lost overboard from a fishing smack were extremely high, mainly because the crew spent most of their time on deck in bad weather. This was because the cabin was in these conditions a most inhospitable place—the stove would be out, water would be swilling about everywhere, and no comfort would be found. Two men would man the tiller, keeping the vessel's bow into the weather, while the rest of the crew hung on wherever they could. When a particularly big sea was seen to be approaching, the cry "Watter" would ring out, and the crew—save the helmsmen—would dive down the companionway for safety. Those who didn't manage to get below in time would find themselves standing in a wall of water, sweeping the length of the deck and carrying away anything not already made fast. Anyone swept over the stern this way stood almost no chance at all of being picked up again, especially at night. By the time the smack had been brought about, the victim would invariably have succumbed to the waves. During the 1880 storm, at least fifteen men had gone over the side this way from various fishing vessels.

The year 1880 really marked the turning point in the rise of the sail-powered fishing vessel, for this was the time when steam fishing vessels began to appear. Strangely perhaps, it was three years after this date when the worst disaster of all befell the sailing trawlers off the Yorkshire Coast. It happened early in March 1883, when hundreds of smacks from all parts of the East Coast were working on or near the Dogger Bank. For several days the weather had been calm, with a light north-westerly breeze. About midnight on 5 March, however, a storm burst suddenly, and the seas rose with frightening speed. Chaos reigned over the whole area, many men died on that awful night, and when daylight came a scene of desolation was all around. Disabled smacks were everywhere, the water was littered with wreckage, and still the sea foamed and the wind howled. The storm lasted for several days, and when it eventually blew itself out it was found that more than 250 men had died; 43 smacks had been sunk, 38 seriously damaged and 51 others had suffered some damage. Of those men who survived the storm, many had been so shaken by the experience that they never went to sea again.

In most cases, it was not known just how, when or even where the smacks were lost. The Scarborough smack *Cornelia*, for instance, had been at sea throughout the storm, and it was not until 22 March that the *Scarborough Gazette* reported, "Hope has now been given up . . ." Six days later, part of the stern of a boat was washed up at Blakeney in Norfolk. It was painted black and red, and written on it in white paint were the words "Cornelia SH 93". No trace was found of the five crew.

A strange coincidence occurred at Scarborough as a result of this awe-inspiring storm, beginning with the safe arrival of the Hartlepool keelboat *Thomas Davison*. She reported that during the storm Mr. Webster, her skipper, had been lost overboard. About a quarter of a mile south of the harbour, the Liverpool keelboat *Active* drove ashore and became a total wreck. The six crew were saved, including Webster, the skipper—son of the late skipper of the *Thomas Davison*. Also ashore some distance away was the Hartlepool steam trawler *Maybird*, another victim of the storm. Her crew of six were taken off, and her skipper was a man named Webster, uncle of the *Active's* skipper and brother of the late skipper of the *Thomas Davison*.

The men who crewed these sailing trawlers were noted for their fearlessness, and in some cases for their recklessness. One famous old-world skipper at Scarborough rejoiced in the name of "Mad Isaac", and not without reason as the following story illustrates. When bad weather made Scarborough harbour-mouth impassable, a flag was flown by day and a beacon lit by night to warn smacks not to try and enter. This practice was known as "burning off" the trawlers. When Mad Isaac was burnt off, however, he defied the warning, no doubt being eager to reach the warmth of his fireside. He made a reckless dash for the harbour mouth, but an enormous sea picked up his smack, carried her **over the top** of the outer pier, and dumped her squarely in the harbour! No doubt he claimed later that he had made this fantastic entry purposely! Another man of this ilk was John Donkin, skipper of a Scarborough coble. His penchant was to fight his way out of the harbour in terrible weather in order to lie in the bight of the outer pier, where he awaited the opportunity to earn money through pilotage or salvage. The place where he waited is known to this day as "John Donkin's Bight".

Other smacksmen were noted for a less endearing quality, namely extreme cruelty. One of the most widely publicised incidents of this kind involved the skipper of the smack *Rising Sun*, for his cruelty resulted in murder. Skipper Osmond Otto Brand had a burning hatred of his cook and cabin boy, a youth of 14 named William Pappers of Hull, and he made no attempts to conceal his hatred. During a voyage in 1882, the boy was subjected to the most appalling cruelty: he was beaten with ropes and iron bars, was drenched repeatedly with icy water thrown at his naked body, and was beaten up generally almost daily. Eventually, the boy died and his body was dumped over the side. The crew were instructed to tell the authorities that he had fallen overboard after being struck by the mainsail—and this was quite feasible, for it did happen often. However, one crew-member must have had a conscience at least, for the incident eventually came to light, and Brand was arrested. His trial caused angry scenes at the courthouse, and the public made it clear that they wished to see him hanged. On 11 May, Brand was sentenced to death, and despite his pleading innocent to the end, the sentence was carried out in Leeds.

In April 1883 a case was brought at Grimsby Police Court against the skipper and two hands of the smack *Young Alfred*, for "brutal and even murderous treatment of Charles Newton, a fourteen year old Scarborough lad on a trial trip to sea". The crew had in fact tied ropes round the boy and hoisted him to the masthead on a lantern halyard. On another occasion, a rope was tied round his neck, and he was dumped overboard. Afterwards he was sent below, with a potato sack wrapped around him. He was ill-treated in various other ways before the voyage ended, yet when questioned by the magistrates Newton said that he "liked the sea well enough". On looking into the boy's background, it was found that he had a "thoroughly bad character". He had on several occasions absconded from the workhouse, where he had been sent after being convicted of stealing a bather's boots and stockings at Scarborough. The poor wretch was described as being "rather dull, undersized and weakly". These were not isolated incidents; many cases of cruelty came to light after this, and there were other murders aboard fishing smacks, despite the outcome of the Brand case.

Sometimes the dangers inherent in their way of life weighed heavily on the minds of smacksmen, but generally it was rare for them to adopt a new life ashore; there is much truth in the saying "once a fisherman always a fisherman". There were occasions though when a smacksman would find the thought of putting to sea for six weeks or more just too much to face, and cases of last-minute "desertion" have been recorded. This happened the day before Good Friday of 1871 at Scarborough, when the smack *Contrast* was to leave for the fishing grounds. Two of the crew, John Edwards and Fred. Greaves, failed to appear at the appointed time, and they were subsequently required to appear before the Scarborough magistrates—several of whom, incidentally, were smack owners. The two men were sentenced to one month's hard labour for their "crime", even though, ironically, one of them did not appear at the trial—because he had gone to sea!

Many smacksmen sought consolation in strong liquor, though as many more were very religious men who shunned this form of "Dutch courage". In April of 1869, a hundred smacks or more left Hull on one tide, and newspapers of the time noted that of the 500 men and boys aboard at the time of sailing, not one was drunk, and the smacks carried no liquor. However, there were many Dutch "copers" in the North Sea; vessels whose sole purpose was to sell tobacco and liquor to fishermen, who were glad to pay exorbitant rates for these comforts after several weeks at sea without them. Many of the more sober smack skippers considered the copers to be a great evil, and would have had them "swept from the face of the sea" had they been able.

By the mid 1890s, smacks were rapidly disappearing from the

North Sea as the steam trawler became more widespread in use. Hull, for instance, had 448 smacks in 1887, but by 1893 there was none. In the years between 1880 and the outbreak of World War I, approximately 1,000 sailing trawlers had been sunk by stranding, collision, fire or foundering.

THREE SCORE AND TEN

And it's three score and ten, boys and men, were lost from Grimsby town,
From Yarmouth down to Scarborough, many hundreds more were drowned,
Our herring craft our trawlers, our fishing smacks as well,
They long defied the bitter night and battled with the swell.

Methinks I see a host of craft, spreading their sails with ease,
As down the Humber they do glide, all bound for the Northern Seas,
Methinks I see on each small craft, a crew with hearts so brave,
Going out to earn their daily bread upon the restless wave.

Chorus

Methinks I see them yet again as they leave the land behind,
Casting their nets into the sea, the herring shoals to find,
Methinks I see them yet again and the're all on board all right,
With their sails close reefed and their decks cleaned up, and their side lights burning bright.

Chorus

October's night brought such a sight you've never seen before,
There was masts and yards and broken spars, come washed up on the shore,
There was many a heart of sorrow, there was many a heart so brave,
There was many a fine and hearty lad did find a watery grave.

Chorus

(This folk song tells, rather inaccurately, of the storm of March 1883).

3.   Paddle Trawlers

EARLY in the 1800s steam paddle boats began to appear on many British waterways, but they were not generally well received by seamen. Steamers were regarded as being ugly, dirty and unreliable, and were little more than the playthings of scientists as far as seamen were concerned. However, one or two of the experimental steamboats—notably the *Charlotte Dundas* of 1801 and the *Comet* of 1812—had enough success to prove that there was a future for steamships.

In 1814 two paddle steamers were put into service on the Tyne, but after two years the owners admitted failure, and the boats were laid up. A second attempt to run a passenger service using one of these paddlers was made later, but this too failed. Finally, in 1818, one of the Tyne steam paddlers was used to tow a sailing ship for a distance of thirteen miles, against the wind, proving its worth at last. Three years later there were fourteen paddlers on the Tyne, all working as tugboats, and the pattern was established. Before very long, hundreds of paddle tugs were in use in all the major ports.

The *Scarborough Gazette* of 28 August 1873 carried a story which read: "The visit of the sailing and steam yacht *Dewdrop* opens the question here as it has done elsewhere, of the desirability of applying steam as a locomotive agency to our fishing craft . . ." The *Dewdrop* was in fact a sailing boat with an auxiliary steam engine, and it showed fishermen that it was possible to fit a steam engine into an existing boat—it was not necessary to have a steamboat specially built for the job. The owner of the *Dewdrop*, a Mr. Leach, showed off his vessel by visiting fishing boats while they were at work on the seas.

By the second half of the nineteenth century, steamboats were becoming more widespread in use, and some of the early paddle tugs found themselves without sufficient work. Rather than have them lie idle, their owners allowed paddle tugs to be used for towing fishing smacks to and from the open sea. On days when there was little or no wind, smack skippers sometimes took advantage of the paddlers by shooting their nets while still under tow, and they found that they could trawl successfully this way. The next step in

23

the development of the paddle trawler seems, in retrospect, an obvious one—dispense with the smack, and let the paddler pull the beam trawl. It was not until 1877, however, that William Purdy of North Shields announced his intention of doing just this, much to the derision of the fishing community. Nothing daunted, Purdy went ahead, and his ancient tug *Messenger* met with a considerable degree of success as a trawler, using the same type of beam trawl that was pulled by sailing trawlers. Soon paddle tugs were being bought up and equipped as trawlers at various places, but notably at Shields, Sunderland and Scarborough.

The first real mention of steam paddle trawlers at Scarborough came in December of 1880, when the local paper reported: "There were in the harbour on Tuesday several vessels of a novel fleet, viz. steam trawlers, several of which were of considerable power". The fleet referred to consisted of a number of ex-tugboats from the North-East ports, and local fishermen were not slow to note that one of the vessels caught over £80 worth of fish in the first 24 hours of its time at Scarborough. Inevitably, a number of Scarborough boat owners began making negotiations of their own and, before the month was out, the port could boast two paddle trawlers. First to arrive was the *Dandy*, an old tug bought from Liverpool by Messrs. Ness, Wyrill and Woodall. Built in 1863, the *Dandy* was an iron vessel of 126 tons gross and 106 feet long. By coincidence, but very appropriately, she was given the fishing number SH 1. On the same day, the paddle trawler *Tuskar* arrived, bought from Cardiff by Mr. McBean.

The *Dandy* did not have a very auspicious beginning to her life at Scarborough. On her first trip, a crewman named James Field was killed when a chain snapped during the hauling of the net, and on her return to port, the vessel smashed into the pier and damaged one of her paddle-boxes. However, these mishaps proved no deterrent, and several more paddlers arrived with each month. The "going price" for a paddle trawler at this time was between £2,000 and £3,000 with gear.

Early in 1882 the paddle trawler *Knight of the Cross* arrived at Scarborough, to become the largest of the new fleet. This vessel had formerly been a tender to a larger vessel at Liverpool, and hence was licensed to carry passengers. Unable to resist the chance that this gave, the owners ran a "pleasure trip" in their new boat when it arrived, though "pleasure" was hardly the appropriate word in the event! The sea was so rough during the trip that the dignitaries aboard the *Knight of the Cross* were unable to enjoy the voyage through sea-sickness and an "abundant and well-prepared luncheon went untasted". No doubt the owners and their wealthy friends would be only too glad to hand the vessel over to the men who were going to run her as a fishing boat after this! However, later in the year, the newly formed Britannia Steam

Shipping Company of Scarborough announced its intention of using one of its paddlers as a fishing boat in winter, and a pleasure boat in summer.

Smack owners did not fear the advent of paddle trawlers, for they were not in competition with them. Paddlers were only suitable for inshore fishing; they carried no ice, and stayed at sea for only two days or so before landing their catch. Smacks on the other hand fished well off shore, and remained at sea for much longer

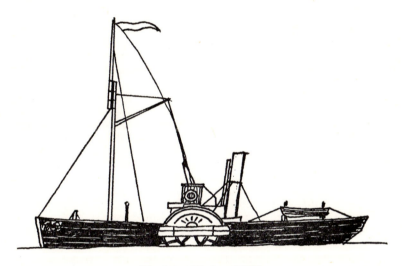

Wooden paddle tug of 1880

periods. Relations between the two types of craft were not always smooth, however; on 20 December, 1883 a Royal Commission on Trawl Fishing was held at Scarborough, and many local smacksmen voiced strong complaints. George Verrill, a Staithes fisherman, declared that steam trawlers had done more damage to fish stocks in five years than smacks had done in fifteen. Many other smacksmen backed up this statement in an attempt to have restrictions placed on the "new-fangled" steam trawlers. The smacksmen were, of course, fighting a losing battle, but it was screw-trawlers and not paddlers that were to put them out of business eventually. One observer at the time said of those who objected to steam trawlers: "Fishermen are unfortunately subject to two great failings—they are never contented with their own luck, and they are always jealous of the luck of their neighbours." It was noticeable in fact that all the complaints came from fishing ports which for one reason or another had no steam paddle trawlers.

One thing that paddle trawlers and smacks had in common was their vulnerability to bad weather, and many of them in fact came to grief. The storm of October 1880 that claimed several smacks was also responsible for sinking the North Shields paddle trawler *Nation's Hope*, which went down with all hands off Port Mulgrave. Another early victim was the 104 ton iron built *Chevy Chase*, a Sunderland paddle-trawler. She left her home port on 4 October 1886, under the command of Henry Thompson. Two days later, while steaming through dense fog, she struck a submerged reef called Old Horse Rocks, off Gristhorpe. Five vessels had already been totally wrecked on this same reef during the preceding twenty-one years; the *Chevy Chase* became number six. The skipper and eight crew were saved however; they took to the boats, were subsequently picked up by a Filey coble, and were landed safely. The vessel, owned by a Mrs. Nicholson, was insured for the sum of £1,500.

Three years later, on 7 October 1889, the North Shields paddle trawler *Alpha* suffered the ignominy of being run down and sunk by a sailing vessel, some fifteen miles off Spurn Point. The collision took place during a stiff south-westerly gale, just after midnight, and for a while the two vessels were interlocked. It was clear that the *Alpha* had suffered severe damage, so her crew and skipper Brown clambered aboard the sailing vessel, which proved to be the schooner *Lottie* of Padstow, bound for the Tyne with phosphates. Soon the vessels drifted apart, and the *Alpha* foundered within the hour. The *Lottie* had not escaped unscathed, so made for Scarborough, where she landed the shipwrecked crew of the *Alpha*.

Heavy seas alone were the undoing of the Cardiff paddle trawler *Marie Joseph*. She was fishing off Scarborough on the night of 11 November 1891 when the weather began to worsen. Before long, the violent pitching and tossing that she received caused her wooden planking to spring, and the vessel made water rapidly. The crew pumped manfully, but the water in the hold gained on them all the time, and distress signals were hoisted. Fortunately the Scarborough paddler *Star* was close at hand, and the master, F. Goodwill, took immediate action. Using a trawl-warp, he took the *Marie Joseph* in tow and began the long haul through the night to safety. Violent seas kept pushing the vessels apart, and the tow-rope broke but was re-fastened. Eventually, water in the *Marie Joseph* reached the engines, and W. Salmon, the skipper decided that the vessel was doomed. With great difficulty, he and his crew boarded the *Star*, leaving the fifteen year old *Marie Joseph* sinking fast, about two miles north-east of Scarborough.

On 13 December 1893, Scarborough paddle trawler owner W. T. Sellers received from Shields a telegram which read, "Been in collision—boat lost, crew all right". The *Lord Clyde* had left Scarborough on the afternoon of Monday 11 December, heading for an area known to fishermen as "the Garden", some fifteen miles east by north of the town. They had been trawling for some time when darkness fell over the calm sea and five of the crew went below to eat, in readiness for the hauling and gutting which was to come. Two men, Royal Flemings and Thomas Williamson remained on deck, a pleasant enough job for the night was fine, the stars shone brightly and visibility was good. The *Lord Clyde* was moving so slowly that an observer might have thought her stationary; the heavy beam trawl dragging over the sea bed kept her speed down. One of the watchmen noticed a steamer was coming from the north, and suddenly realised that it was bearing down on them, apparently unaware of the trawler's presence. Quickly he raised the alarm and the crew of the *Lord Clyde* scrambled on deck. Hardly had they achieved this when the steamer's bow ripped into the trawler's starboard side, cutting right through to the foot of the mast.

Skipper Hodds, William Snowball and William Nightingale clambered onto the bows of the steamer, which was the *Aberdeen*, a collier from Aberdeen. The four remaining trawler hands, William Cox, Jack Harrison, Williamson and Flemings, were thrown overboard by the impact. Three of them had managed to don life-jackets, but Jack Harrison was without one, and he was not a good swimmer. The *Lord Clyde* was sinking rapidly, and within ten minutes of the impact was gone, causing a strong suction as she sank. Fortunately the four men in the water were able to keep clear of the whirlpool so caused, but they were beginning to suffer from exposure. Harrison managed to grasp the trawler's small boat which, though waterlogged, was still afloat. William Cox, the second hand of the *Lord Clyde*, did his best to "cheer up" the other three, whose strength was waning rapidly in the bitterly cold water. All four were eventually picked up by boats from the *Aberdeen* after they had spent twenty minutes or so struggling in the water. Once aboard the *Aberdeen*, however, they were treated kindly, and recovered very quickly from the shock they had received. Skipper Hodds wanted the captain of the *Aberdeen* to land them at Scarborough, but as the steamer had sustained considerable damage herself he put her head for the Tyne, from whence he had come the previous day.

They docked at South Shields at 10 a.m. the following morning, and the shipwrecked crew, bereft of everything but their clothes, made their way to the Seaman's Institute. Here they were received with "scant courtesy", and were directed to the agent of the Fishermen's and Shipwrecked Mariners' Society, to which some of them belonged. They found this worthy conducting an auction sale, and were asked to wait until this finished at 4 p.m.! Hodds and his weary crew declined, and made their way across the river to North Shields, where at last they were well received by that Seaman's Institute. They were given the travel warrants they sought, and finally arrived home, to the joy of their relatives, some twenty-four hours after the shipwreck. The *Lord Clyde* was built at Cork in 1864, and had been fishing from Scarborough for eleven years. She was 103 ft. long, of 115 tons gross and was valued at £3,500.

Possibly the most unusual paddle trawler loss was that of the 97 ton *Tuskar* of Scarborough, for she virtually sank herself! She was fishing off the town on 6 January 1895, and all went well until 1-30 a.m. the following morning when the crew found that the net was so heavy that they could barely lift it from the sea. Unfortunately it was not an exceptionally good catch of fish; the *Tuskar* had picked up a huge stone, which they estimated to weigh half-a-ton. The stone would not pass through the cod-end of the net, so they had two alternatives, either the net had to be cut away, or the stone had to be landed on the deck, disentangled and lifted over the side. They opted for the latter course, and efforts were made to get the stone aboard. Meanwhile the stone was swinging to and fro with the motion of the ship, and when a big sea passed under them, the heavy roll of the ship caused a longer swing, and the stone smashed into the trawler's hull with a sickening thud. This sprang out one of the plates, and the *Tuskar* began to fill. The crew pumped for thirty minutes but had to abandon ship in their small boat when the *Tuskar* began to settle fast. After a very unpleasant time among the heavy seas and the darkness, the seven men were picked up by the Grimsby smack *Reliance*, and were landed at Scarborough on Monday night. Built at Low Walker in 1870, the *Tuskar* fished as SH. 45 and was owned by Appleby and Brogden.

The same company lost another paddle trawler some three years later, when the 67 tons *Spurn* was run down by the German steamer *Gemma* some fourteen miles off Whitby. Skipper Frank Eden of the *Spurn* saw the steamer bearing down on them on the night of 28 October 1898, but was powerless to avert the collision. The *Gemma* struck the *Spurn* in her paddle box, and she began to fill at once. The seven crew were able to scramble aboard the steamer minutes before the *Spurn* went down; they were later transferred to the Hull vessel *Electra* which landed them at Scarborough. This incident was in many ways similar to that involving the *Lord Clyde* some five years earlier. On both occasions the weather was clear, and both trawlers claimed that their lights were burning brightly. It seems in retrospect that the steamers must have been at fault, if we accept that the paddlers were indeed showing lights. The only consolation is that no lives were lost in either case.

Next of the paddle trawlers to come to grief off the Yorkshire coast was the 100 ton *Fearless* owned by John Ness of Scarborough. She was returning home from the fishing grounds in dense fog on

Tuesday 30th April, 1901 when she struck Blea Wyke Nab, south of Robin Hood's Bay. The crew took to the boat when they found the engine room full of water, and rowed to Scarborough, a distance of over ten miles. As soon as the news was made known, the Scarborough steamer *Admiral* set off to inspect the wreck. They found that as the trawler had stranded at high tide, she was left high and dry when the water receded. Two large rocks had penetrated the hull, so the stores and catch were removed, and the *Fearless* was abandoned as a total wreck.

By the beginning of the twentieth century, steam paddle trawlers were already outdated, and one writer said in 1904 that they were then obsolete, and could be seen only at Scarborough and one or two other ports. Scarborough's last paddle trawler was in fact the *Constance*, purpose built at North Shields in 1882. She was wrecked at Hartlepool on 22 March 1910, bringing the history of these fascinating little ships to an end.

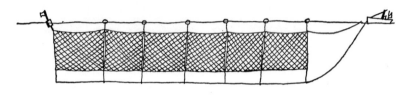

Herring drift net

4.   Screw-Steam Trawlers

As early as the mid-1850s, attempts had been made to fit steam engines and screw propellors into sailing fishing vessels, but none had had a great deal of success. Indeed, it was not unknown for a skipper to fit a steam engine, find that he didn't like it, and have it removed again. This was an expensive experiment, and no doubt the sight of this happening once would deter many others who fancied their chances at screw-steam trawling. As we have seen, the steam paddle trawler proved quite a success, and no doubt this too slowed down the development of screw trawlers. However, screw-powered vessels were a distinct success in other types of craft, and it was inevitable that sooner or later screw trawlers had to come. In 1878, the *Scarborough Gazette* had made the forecast that "steam-trawling will lead to an almost infinite future in the history of deep-sea fishing". Incidentally, the same article went on to say, "The real truth is that the sea is for all intents and purposes inexhaustible"! A pity that the reporter could not meet one of today's inshore fishermen to discuss this statement!

One of the first vessels specifically built as a screw trawler—in fact probably the first—was the aptly named *Pioneer,* an iron vessel of 94 feet length. She was built for James Sellers and others of Scarborough in November 1881, and was widely admired on her arrival. The *Pioneer* was fitted with steam-winches and capstan, but significantly she also carried sails, being schooner-rigged. Sellers, who was to command the boat personally, was leaving nothing to chance! At about the same time the Grimsby and North Sea Steam Trawling Company was formed to launch the screw trawler *Zodiac,* at a cost of £3,500. These vessels were quickly followed by others, and all were successful right from the start.

The appearance of the screw trawler was to mark the end of an era, for it could do all that a smack could do and more, with greater efficiency, and more profitably. The days of the sailing trawler were numbered, and so too were the days when a fisherman could own and work his own boat. Screw trawlers were normally outside the pocket of individual fishermen, and so steam fishing companies were set up in the major fishing ports. All sorts of unlikely land-lubbers had a financial interest in these companies, no doubt aware of the rich rewards that were waiting to be reaped.

In 1891, the first steam trawler visited Iceland, and within a few years regular visits were being made to the White Sea, and other far off fishing grounds. The North Sea grounds were in any case becoming exhausted by this time, and this was another reason why smacks had to be replaced by a more efficient type of vessel. With the advent of the screw-trawler came also a new method of trawling, one that used wooden boards to keep the nets open instead of the beam that had been used previously. As is the case with many innovations, there is some doubt as to where and when this method was devised, but it is known that Skipper Normandale of Scarborough was a pioneer of it with his screw trawler *Otter*. To this day, the boards that are used to keep the net open are known as

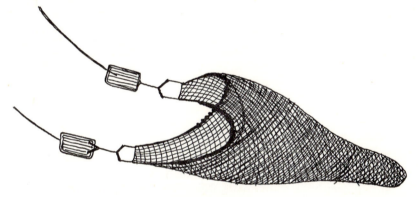

The otter trawl

"Otter-boards". Much difficulty was experienced with this system at first, for they tried to pull both boards and the net using a single warp—only one warp had been needed to pull a beam trawl, after all. However, it was found that if the otter-trawl snagged a submerged object and caught fast, it had the effect of pulling the trawler broadside on, a position no skipper likes to put his vessel in. The problem was eventually solved by using two trawl warps, one to each board. This brought further problems, leading to the development of a winch with two separate drums, which revolved independently. It was many years before the system was finally perfected, but the method of trawling used today is basically the same as that of Skipper Normandale eighty odd years ago.

Inevitably, perhaps, many screw trawlers were wrecked just as the paddlers and the sailing trawlers had been before them, but the reasons were not quite the same. Bad storms were no longer the prime cause of shipwrecks; it was dense fog that skippers now feared most, for this led to collisions at sea and strandings ashore.

One of the first screw steam trawlers to come to grief off the Yorkshire Coast was the 161 ton *Chilian*, owned by the Grimsby Incorporated Box Fishing Company. Her trials were conducted on 27 January 1894, and her first voyage began five days later. The *Chilian* proved to be a remarkably successful vessel, earning high prices which delighted her crew and owners. Little did they know that less than two months later she was destined to be pounded to pieces on the cruel rocks of the Yorkshire Coast.

At 3-00 a.m. on Sunday, 8 April 1894, she was steaming for home after a successful trip to Iceland. Her speed was kept right down, for dense fog had shrouded the Yorkshire Coast for some days, and Captain J. W. Little was tense and anxious. Soundings were taken from time to time and the compass was in constant use, but they had no way of knowing with certainty just where they were. Half an hour later, the *Chilian's* stem crashed with sickening violence on to Filey Brigg. Captain Little sounded a fierce blast on the whistle, for he knew that the Grimsby trawler *Hercules* was following him, and did not wish her to share his fate. The *Chilian's* engines were put full astern, but it was useless; the vessel was struck fast, and was badly damaged in the bows. Water was pouring into the ship at an alarming rate, and the crew had no option but to try and save themselves. In the darkness, five crewmen attempted to launch the ship's boat, but in doing this were lost overboard, and all were drowned. The captain took refuge on the trawler's funnel, several others climbed the rigging, and all was confusion. Fortunately, the *Hercules* had heeded the warning and stood by a short way off. She sent off a search party in her small boat, and after a few hours the remaining crew of the *Chilian* ,including the master, were saved. From a crew of eleven men, only five survived; five had been lost from the ship's boat, and a sixth man, John Barker, had died on the deck, probably as a result of a boom falling across him.

At the inquest some alarming things came to light; the coastguard reported that the bell-buoy off the Brigg end had apparently not been sounding its warning, and guns which had been fired every five minutes from Flamborough Head had also failed to warn off the trawler. Although the local rescue services were called out, it was several hours before they arrived at the scene, long after the survivors had been picked up. At first it was hoped that divers might be able to patch up the holes in the *Chilian*, when she could be pumped out, and refloated. This was not to be, however; the trawler subsequently fell some fifteen feet from a ledge on the Brigg, dislodging some two tons of rock, and totally wrecking herself.

Three years later, the Hull steam trawler *Sleuthhound* met with

Lug rigged sailing cobles in Scarborough's South Bay

Smack *Nymph* (**SH 61**) and herring coble *William* & *Sarah* (**SH 145**) in Scarborough harbour.

Hartlepool fifie *Summer Cloud* and "converter" smacks off Scarborough about 1898

Herring cobles and yawls off Filey about 1890

34

Sailing coble beached in Filey Bay about 1890

Smacksmen enjoying a chat by the harbourside at Scarborough, late nineteenth century

Cobles landing herring from the yawls anchored off Scarborough

Unloading a cargo of ice brought by a schooner from Norway during last century

an almost identical fate, but this time without loss of life. The six year old vessel was returning home with a good catch when, at 7-30 a.m. on 27 October 1897, she struck the extreme end of Filey Brigg in dense fog. She stranded at low tide, which is normally the best time for this to happen—there is always a chance that when the tide rises, the vessel will be floated off. This did not happen however; the rising tide flooded the vessel, and her fate was sealed. Filey fishermen boarded the trawler and carried her catch ashore while the paddle trawlers *Dandy*, *Dunrobin* and *Star* stood by. The Scarborough pleasure boat *Cambria*, another paddler, attempted to tow the *Sleuthhound* off the rocks, but this too failed. The fishing boats, realising that there was nothing they could do, carried on with their work, leaving the *Sleuthhound* to the mercy of the rocks and the waves.

The twentieth century brought with it a great increase in the numbers of steam trawlers, and a corresponding increase in the numbers of wrecks. Fishermen had a theory that the ironstone present in the cliffs at Ravenscar had an adverse affect on ship's compasses, and there was a great deal of evidence to back up their statement—and very expensive evidence at that! On 18 September 1903, two steam trawlers were ashore at the same time here during a fog. One was the Hull trawler *Prime Minister*, which fished out of Scarborough under skipper James Sellers; the other was the *Otter*, skippered by James' cousin, Edward Sellers. The *Prime Minister* broke up where she lay, a little to the south of Hayburn Wyke, but her crew got off safely and were landed at Scarborough. The *Otter* was more fortunate; she was refloated later. This was, incidentally, the same vessel that had pioneered the use of the "otter-trawl" some years earlier, and was later to be sunk by enemy action in September 1916.

Earlier in 1903 this area had claimed the Hull trawler *Puritan* which had run ashore between Peak Point and Blea Wyke Point while homeward bound from Iceland. She broke up very quickly, and large quantities of fish washed up later. Again, no lives were lost; the crew took to the boats and were picked up some hours later by the Scarborough trawler *Hero*. A fourth trawler came to grief here before the year was out; on 15 December 1903, the Hull trawler *Etruria* ran aground in dense fog almost exactly where the *Prime Minister* had been wrecked earlier. The crew were forced to abandon ship, and she became a wreck, as a result of which her skipper was given a three-month suspension. It seems particularly ironic that most of the trawlers that were wrecked on the Yorkshire coast were homeward bound; having faced the dangers of Icelandic waters, they so often came to grief when their voyage was almost at an end and home was nearly in sight.

Although Filey Brigg and Robin Hood's Bay - Ravenscar were real danger zones, there was and is an even greater hazard to the

Screw-steam trawler of 1886

south—the jutting cliffs of Flamborough Head. Countless vessels have been wrecked here over the years, and literally dozens of steam trawlers have stranded here at one time or another. At least twelve trawlers have been totally wrecked at the foot of these cliffs, and the remains of many of them are visible to this day, if you know where to look.

A tragic wreck occurred on 12 April 1902, when the 144 ton Grimsby steam trawler *Tynemouth* struck the foot of Bempton Cliffs during dense fog. The disaster occurred during the night, and when she was first seen on the following morning the crew were beyond help. The vessel was lying broadside on, with her deck facing the cliff, and two or three bodies could be seen floating nearby. There were no survivors. At the point where the ship had struck, the cliffs drop sheer into the sea; there was nowhere that they could have got ashore.

Another great tragedy took place not far from here some thirty-three years later when the Hull trawler *Skegness* was driven ashore with the loss of eleven lives. The news of the first signs of impending danger was received on the night of 24 September 1935 by a trawler skipper in Scarborough who was at home listening to his radio. He hurried down to his own vessel in the harbour in order to transmit a reply. At this time, the master of the *Skegness* reported that he had run ashore while homeward bound from the Faroes, but did not require assistance; though it was raining heavily the sea was calm, and the cliffs protected the vessel from the light south-westerly wind.

Conditions rapidly worsened, however; an hour later there was

Screw-steam trawler of 1910

a heavy north-easterly gale blowing, bringing with it heavy seas and driving rain. The skipper of the *Skegness* now asked for the assistance of the lifeboat—but was unable to tell them just where he was. In the darkness, it was impossible for the crew of the stricken vessel to identify the cliffs above them. At 11-10 p.m. Scarborough lifeboat was launched, and she searched her stretch of coastline, as far south as Filey, returning to her base at 2-00 a.m. Flamborough and Filey lifeboats had also been launched, and the Speeton rocket brigade had been alerted. Just after midnight, the rocket brigade located the wreck and attempted to make contact with her, 400 feet below. The rockets were, however, blown back by the wind, which was so strong by this time that the men had to crawl on all fours to the cliff edge. Both lifeboats were cruising up and down offshore, but could not see the trawler, and finally returned home at 3 a.m. The clifftop party had by now rigged up a searchlight, which showed that there was no sign of life aboard the wreck. At 4-30 a.m. Scarborough and Flamborough lifeboats were again called out, and this time they located the trawler, only to find that her funnel and wheelhouse had gone, and her eleven crew had drowned.

Less than two years later, the Grimsby steam trawler *Lord Ernle* suffered a similar fate, but with less tragic results. She was returning from the White Sea, when at 10 o'clock on the night of 2 March 1937 she struck rocks about a mile south of the wreck of the *Skegness*. Her crew, who had been playing cards in the cabin, felt the vessel shiver from stem to stern, and rushed on deck. They could dimly see the cliffs towering above them, as the trawler lurched over the submerged rocks, her engines racing astern. A "Mayday" call was sent out, and fire was kindled on the whaleback bow in order that rescuers would see them. Within thirty minutes the Flamborough lifeboat was at sea, and at midnight she came up with the *Lord Ernle*, whose stern was now underwater, while her bows touched the sheer cliffs. A heavy ground swell prevented the lifeboat from getting close to the wreck, so she anchored, and veered down as close as she could get. A line was fired across the wreck and one trawlerman was safely hauled aboard the lifeboat. Twice the line parted, and was made fast again, as one by one the crewmen were saved. As the rescue proceeded, the fires on the trawler died away, and they worked in pitch darkness until the coastguard arrived on the clifftop with a searchlight. At one stage a heavy sea picked up the lifeboat and flung her onto the deck of the trawler, but fortunately she slid off again, though half her rudder was torn away. Three hours passed altogether before the skipper of the *Lord Ernle* was saved, the last of the fifteen men to leave the trawler. The lifeboat had been at sea for four-and-a-half hours when she finally reached home in safety, having achieved a magnificent rescue for which Coxswain George Leng was awarded the Silver Medal for gallantry.

Normally, steam powered fishing boats could cope with gales and storms without too much difficulty, but from time to time they would be overcome in just the same way that the old smacks had been before them. On 25 November 1925 a raging blizzard whipped up the seas in Bridlington Bay, causing great white surf to spread over the Smethwick Sands, a huge sandbar that lies to the north and east of the town. A steam drifter was coming from the north, obviously making for the harbour at Bridlington, when three huge waves crashed over the vessel. Men could be seen scrambling into the rigging as the disabled vessel began to sink, but in a few minutes it was all over and the steamer was engulfed with all on board. It was some time before the identity of the vessel was known, but subsequent events proved her to be the *Research*, owned by T. Melrose and Sons of Hull and managed by the Filey United Steam Trawling Co. Particularly tragic was the fact that among those lost were five members of one Filey family.

It is not often that a lifeboat rescues the crew of one vessel twice in two days, but this happened in the case of the wreck of the Grimsby trawler *Saltaire*. She ran aground during an easterly gale on the Binks, a sandbank to the east of Spurn Point, on 10 October 1939. The crew were rescued by the lifeboat, and the *Saltaire* drifted off the sandbank and grounded again on the mainland. At low tide the crew were able to reboard in the hope of refloating the vessel, but heavy weather caused the seas to rise again and they had to be rescued for a second time. Because of the difficulty of this, the lifeboat Coxswain was awarded the R.N.L.I. Silver Bar. The *Saltaire*, a twenty year old vessel of 202 tons, was not refloated; her wreck can be seen at Spurn to this day, high and dry on the beach at low tide.

One of the last steam trawlers to be wrecked off the Yorkshire Coast was the *Aucuba*, a Grimsby trawler of 211 tons built at Beverley in 1906. Forty five years later, on 5 September 1951, she was involved in a collision with the Italian steamer *Maria Biblioni* some eleven miles east of Robin Hood's Bay. The crew of eleven boarded the steamer and left the *Aucuba* in a sinking condition. Tugs that went out to try and salvage the trawler failed to find her; she now lies rusting away on the seabed somewhere off the North Yorkshire coast, along with the thousands of other wrecks there.

5.   Fishermen at War

When Britain entered World War I, the Germans knew that if they were to succeed they must first destroy Britain's dominance on the sea. Accordingly, they launched a massive mine-laying programme in an attempt to make all England's seaways impassable —this would not only damage our own shipping, but would also dissuade neutral vessels from bringing much needed supplies here. During the course of the war the Germans laid more than forty thousand mines, of which a great proportion were in the North Sea.

Fortunately for us, Admiral Lord Charles Beresford had foreseen the possibility of this happening, and after a visit to East Coast ports in 1907 he recommended the use of steam trawlers as mine-sweepers in the event of war. Admiral Beresford pointed out that in wartime, trawlers would not be able to fish anyway, and using them as mine sweepers would free naval vessels for other duties. On top of this, fishermen were undoubtedly the best men for the dangerous job of mine-sweeping, for they were used to handling wires and trawls and they knew the coastline of the North Sea very well. As a result of the decision that was taken, the rank of "Skipper RNR" was to appear in navy lists for the first time.

On 16 December 1914, Vice-Admiral Hipper led a German battle-cruiser squadron which bombarded the towns of Hartlepool, Whitby and Scarborough, killing 120 people and wounding 400 others. During the attack on Scarborough, the 4,350 ton *Kolberg* laid a hundred mines close inshore between Scarborough and Filey, making this the densest minefield that had been known anywhere in the world. It proved to be frighteningly effective; three cargo ships struck mines and sank south-east of Scarborough within hours of the *Kolberg's* departure. Orders were given for the clearance of the minefield, and on 18 December a fleet of Grimsby minesweeping-trawlers was seen steaming into the danger zone as dawn broke.

It was a beautifully clear morning as the trawlers went about their deadly work, pouring dense black smoke from their funnels into the clear sky. At 8-00 a.m. they were off Cayton Bay, with their sweeps streaming out to cut the wires that anchored the mines to the seabed. Within five minutes, eighteen mines had been exploded, and the senior officer realised that this was the densest minefield

42

he had ever seen. As the work proceeded the tide fell rapidly, and this of course brought the mines nearer to the bottoms of the trawlers. Before long the inevitable happened and one trawler, the leading vessel, struck a mine. A huge hole was blown in her port bow, but she did not sink because of her size; she was the largest trawler that local people had seen. After drifting inshore the *Passing*, as she was called, was taken in tow and was safely berthed in Scarborough harbour.

At 11-00 a.m. a second vessel, the 273 ton *Orianda*, was blown up while steaming at full speed. Unable to stop, she careered on through the water, sinking as she went. One man went down with the ship; the remainder, including skipper Lieutenant H. B. Boothby RNR, abandoned ship and were rescued by a paddle steamer. Operations were suspended after this until the next day, when the 203 ton trawler *Garmo* was blown up and sunk with the loss of six lives south of Cayton Bay. On Christmas Day 1914 a third minesweeping trawler, the 287 ton *Nighthawk*, struck one of the *Kolberg's* mines and sank in ten seconds. Amazingly, seven of the thirteen crew were saved, largely thanks to the action taken by her skipper Sub-Lieutenant W. Senior. After being in the freezing water for some time he managed to reach a raft, and boarding this, he sculled round using his hands as paddles, picking up his shipmates.

During 1973 one of the local inshore trawlers working off Scarborough fouled her nets on an underwater obstruction, and when they were hauled a large piece of rusty steel was seen to be caught in them. The obstruction broke up before it could be brought aboard, and part of the steel fell back into the depths, but not before the crew had recognised their "catch". They knew beyond doubt that they had trawled up a part of the bow of a steam trawler, and the piece that remained in the net was examined carefully. On the rusty steel were some brass letters, reading "NIGH . . .", the rest had broken away. By an amazing coincidence they had trawled up a part of the bow of the ill-fated trawler *Nighthawk*. The find can be seen today in a small but fascinating museum situated at Scalby Mills, Scarborough.

The next steam trawler to come to grief in the Scarborough minefield was minesweeper no. 450 the *Banyers*. Six men died when she blew up, but among the survivors was skipper H. B. Boothby who, it will be remembered, had already been blown up once here a matter of weeks before. On this occasion he escaped by climbing out through the wheelhouse window shortly before the trawler sank. Like the *Orianda*, the *Banyers* was almost a new ship, having been built in 1914.

It should perhaps be mentioned here that during World War 1, 214 minesweepers were lost; roughly one per week for the whole period of the war. Each time one of these vessels sank, on average half of the crew died. Hull and Grimsby between them supplied

43

some 800 trawlers and 9,000 men to defend their country during the war.. Of the mines that were originally laid off Scarborough, 53 were swept up in a month, and by 23 April 1915 when sweeping ceased, 69 had been cleared. Many of the other mines had already served their purpose, however; 14 steamships, four minesweepers and two patrol vessels had been sunk by them, and about 100 men had died. After the sweeping had ended, two steam trawlers that were fishing came upon the *Kolberg's* mines and were sunk. The 289 ton Hull trawler *Sapphire* met her end on 1 March 1915, when one man died, and three months later the Scarborough trawler *Condor* was sunk by a mine some seven miles north-east of the town. Skipper Bob Heritage and the entire crew of eight died when the 151 ton vessel went down on 29 May.

Before the menace of the Scarborough minefield had gone, another threat to fishermen had already made its appearance. On 6 May 1915 the Hull steam trawler *Merrie Islington* was fishing some six miles north-east of Whitby when a German submarine surfaced close by. The crew of the trawler, all Scarborough men, were ordered to abandon ship in their own boat, whereupon the U-boat crew planted a bomb on the *Merrie Islington* and sank her. (Her Skipper, Jimmy Walker of Scarborough, was to die some years later when he was blown up while skipper of the steam trawler *Jack Johnson*.) The *Merrie Islington*, a 147 ton vessel, was the first of many fishing vessels to be sunk in this way during the course of the war. Space prevents a mention of all of these, though brief details of many will be found in the appendix. The way in which the Scarborough fleet suffered deserves a mention, however, for the fleet was very nearly wiped out by U-boats.

On 13 July 1916 two Scarborough steam trawlers, the *Florence* and the *Dalhousie*, were captured and sunk by U-boats, approximately ten miles north-north-east of Whitby. This was only the beginning; on 25 September 1916 no less than eleven Scarborough trawlers were sunk by a U-boat some twenty miles north-east of the town. Although the crews were landed safely, they had lost their means of livelihood, for Scarborough was now left with only four trawlers. On the same day, six steam trawlers from other ports met the same fate in the same area, and many others suffered likewise on other parts of the Yorkshire coast.

One particularly interesting U-boat incident occurred off Flamborough Head on 5 May 1917, when a number of herring cobles were fishing in the area. They were in fact sticking their necks out, for they had been told not to fish this area, as it was known to be a favourite hunting ground for U-boats. However, fish was in short supply and prices were good, so many skippers took the risk. On most occasions they were in fact in little danger, and stories are told of U-boat skippers actually talking to fishermen and obtaining fish from them—it was a request that the fishermen would be unlikely

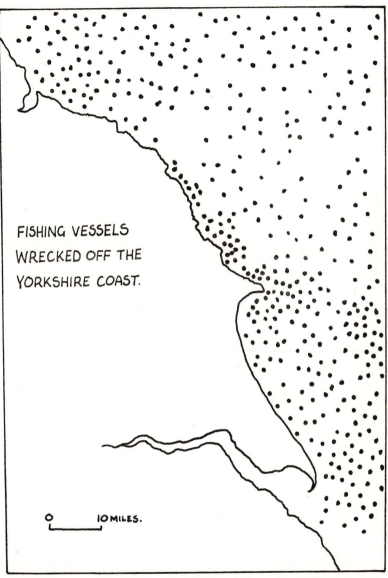

FISHING VESSELS
WRECKED OFF THE
YORKSHIRE COAST.

O   10 MILES.

The general map above indicates all fishing vessel losses; the detail maps on the
following three pages relate to steam fishing vessels only. Positions shown for
offshore wrecks are approximate only.

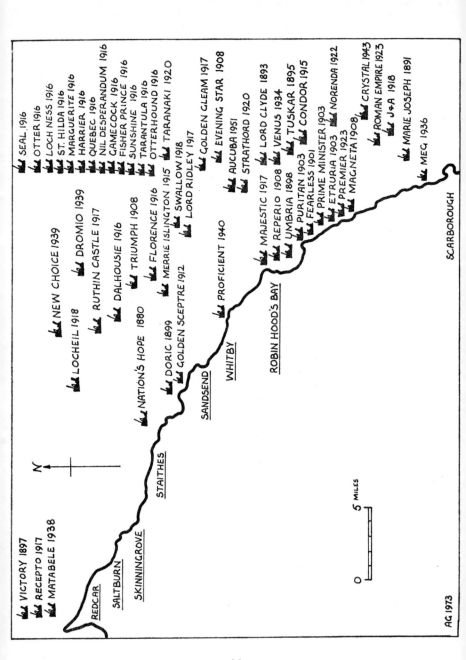

VICTORY 1897
RECEPTO 1917
MATABELE 1938

REDCAR
SALTBURN
SKINNINGROVE
STAITHES

N

SEAL 1916
OTTER 1916
LOCH NESS 1916
ST. HILDA 1916
MARGUERITE 1916
HARRIER 1916
QUEBEC 1916
NIL DESPERANDUM 1916
GAMECOCK 1916
FISHER PRINCE 1916
SUNSHINE 1916
TARANTULA 1916
OTTERHOUND 1916
TARANAKI 1920

GOLDEN GLEAM 1917
EVENING STAR 1908

AUCUBA 1951
STRATHORD 1920

MAJESTIC 1917
REPERIO 1908
UMBRIA 1898
PURITAN 1903
FEARLESS 1901
PRIME MINISTER 1903
ETRURIA 1903
PREMIER 1923
MAGNETA 1908

LORD CLYDE 1893
VENUS 1934
TUSKAR 1895
CONDOR 1915

NORENDA 1922

CRYSTAL 1943
ROMAN EMPIRE 1923
J•A 1918

MARIE JOSEPH 1891

MEG 1936

NEW CHOICE 1939
DROMIO 1939
RUTHIN CASTLE 1917
DALHOUSIE 1916
TRIUMPH 1908
FLORENCE 1916
MERRIE ISLINGTON 1915
SWALLOW 1918
LORD RIDLEY 1917

LOCHEIL 1918

NATION'S HOPE 1880
DORIC 1899
GOLDEN SCEPTRE 1912

PROFICIENT 1940

SANDSEND

WHITBY

ROBIN HOOD'S BAY

SCARBOROUGH

5 MILES

0

AG 1973

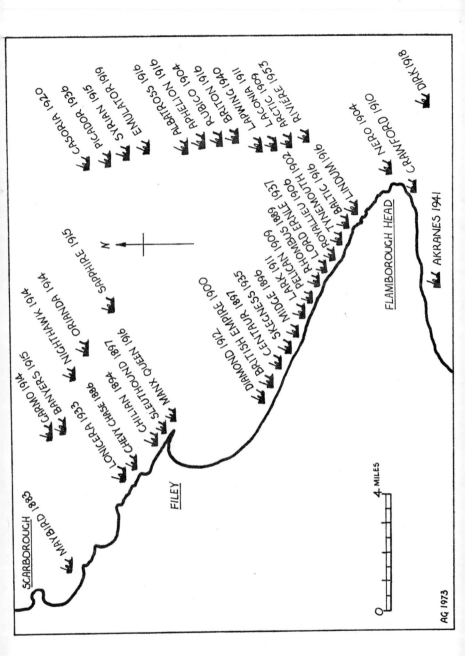

SCARBOROUGH

MAYBIRD 1883

BRABOO 1914
BANKERS 1915
LONICERA 1933
CHEVY CHASE 1886
CHILIAN 1894
SLEUTHOUND 1897
MANX QUEEN 1916

NIGHTHAWK 1914
ORLANDA 1914
SAPPHIRE 1915

FILEY

N

CASSORIA 1920
PICADOR 1936
SYRIAN 1915
EMULATOR 1919

ALBATROSS 1916
APHELION 1916
RUBIO 1904
BRITON 1916
LAPWING 1940
LACONIA 1911
ARCTIC 1953
RIVIERE 1933

DIAMOND 1912
BRITISH EMPIRE 1900
CENTAUR 1897
SKEGNESS 1935
MIDGE 1896
LARK 1911
PELICAN 1909
RHOMBUS 1909
LORD ERNLE 1937
ROYALLIEU 1906
TYNEMOUTH 1906
BALTIC 1916
LINDUM 1916

NERO 1904
CRAWFORD 1910

FLAMBOROUGH HEAD

DIRK 1918

AKRANES 1941

0   4 MILES

AG 1973

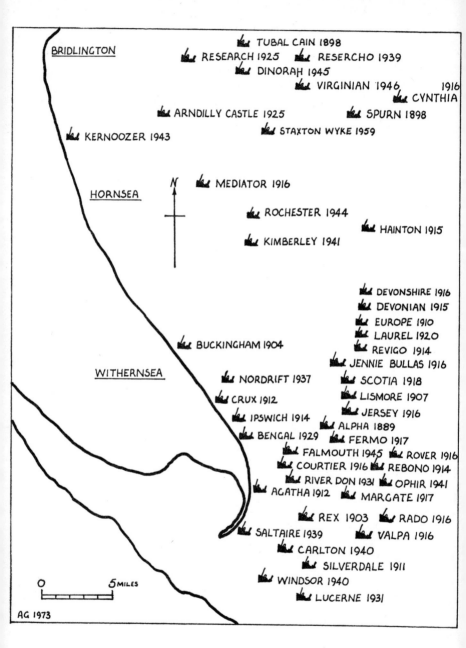

BRIDLINGTON

TUBAL CAIN 1898
RESEARCH 1925   RESERCHO 1939
DINORAH 1945
VIRGINIAN 1946   1916
CYNTHIA
ARNDILLY CASTLE 1925   SPURN 1898
STAXTON WYKE 1959
KERNOOZER 1943

HORNSEA

N

MEDIATOR 1916

ROCHESTER 1944

HAINTON 1915
KIMBERLEY 1941

DEVONSHIRE 1916
DEVONIAN 1915
EUROPE 1910
LAUREL 1920
REVIGO 1914
BUCKINGHAM 1904   JENNIE BULLAS 1916

WITHERNSEA

NORDRIFT 1937   SCOTIA 1918
CRUX 1912   LISMORE 1907
JERSEY 1916
IPSWICH 1914   ALPHA 1889
BENGAL 1929   FERMO 1917
FALMOUTH 1945   ROVER 1916
COURTIER 1916   REBONO 1914
RIVER DON 1931   OPHIR 1941
AGATHA 1912   MARGATE 1917
REX 1903   RADO 1916
SALTAIRE 1939   VALPA 1916
CARLTON 1940
SILVERDALE 1911
WINDSOR 1940
LUCERNE 1931

O   5 MILES

AG 1973

48

to refuse!

On this occasion, however, a U-boat skipper took offence at the name of one of the cobles, the 21 ton *Edith Cavell*, and ordered the crew to leave. (Edith Cavell was a British nurse who was matron of a Belgian clinic—she had been executed by the Germans in 1916 for assisting allied soldiers to escape). He sank the year-old coble and then took the crew aboard the U-boat where he questioned them. The U-boat skipper asked one of the young apprentices where he would have been had he not been at sea that Sunday. "At Sunday school, sir" the boy replied. Apparently the U-boat commander was well-pleased with this reply, and said, "Then I'll see you are there next Sunday". Eventually the crew of the *Edith Cavell* were released, along with some other prisoners, off the Farne Islands. When the crew, all Filey men, arrived back home after some time, half the population of the town turned up at the railway station to receive them! During their "trip" on the U- boat,they had learned that the Germans were also out to get the Scarborough boat *Victory* whose name also upset the U-boat skipper. So seriously was this threat taken that the *Victory* had her name changed at once, and as a double precaution she was sent to another port for the rest of the war.

U-boats did not always have it their own way when they attacked trawlers, however; during 1917 and 1918 many trawlers were armed in order that they could defend themselves. On one occasion a number of trawlers returning from Iceland during the summer of 1918 got the better of a U-boat that attacked them. Later a second group of trawlers was also attacked by a U-boat which fired two torpedoes at them, both of which missed. This was unusual, for torpedoes were expensive, and few could be carried anyway. The U-boat did not even surface; her skipper chose not to engage in a gun battle with the trawlers. Significantly perhaps, in the third year of the war 156 trawlers were sunk by U-boats, but in the fourth year, the number fell to only four.

Mention has already been made of the *Jack Johnson*, a Scarborough steam trawler lost with all hands after striking a mine. What was particularly tragic about this incident is that it took place some time after hostilities had ceased, on 3 September 1920. Unfortunately, this was not an isolated incident. Ten crew of the Scarborough steam trawler *Strathord* died when their vessel was mined and sunk; all hands were lost when the steam drifter *Emulator* met the same fate; and one man died when the *Taranaki* blew up and sank. All of these were Scarborough vessels, and all were lost after the war had ended. A similar fate met the Grimsby trawler *Casoria*, but she was fortunate in that no lives were lost.

Strictly speaking the disaster which befell the Grimsby steam trawler *Lord Airedale* should not be included here, for the tragedy was not due to enemy action, nor was the vessel a total wreck.

However, her story is so tragic that it should perhaps be told. On the night of 18 March 1915 during a violent gale, a flare was seen in Bridlington Bay just south of the town. At once the lifeboat was prepared, and it was dragged on its carriage along the beach for two miles through driving snow. Around midnight, horses pulled the boat on its carriage into the bitterly cold sea. Heavy seas were breaking all around as they crossed a sandbank, and suddenly the lifeboat was lifted and overturned in the raging sea. One man died in the waves, and two horses were killed as the lifeboat carriage was smashed. Despite this tragic beginning the lifeboat was righted, and proceeded towards the stricken vessel, which was minesweeper no 847, the *Lord Airedale*. The lifeboatmen were unable to offer any assistance, however; their small craft was swept past the trawler and was driven helplessly ashore further along the beach, from where it could not be re-launched. A shore rescue party fired rockets to the wreck, which was some 150 yards offshore, but they too failed to make contact. Finally the *Lord Airedale* foundered, and her crew of twelve men died. The vessel was in fact subsequently re-floated, only to be lost the following year when she struck a mine off Harwich.

Altogether in World War 1, 670 fishing vessels were destroyed by enemy action, a truly staggering figure. World War II brought with it yet another menace for fishermen to face, namely attack from the air. On 17 December 1939 five trawlers were bombed off the north-east coast, and four of them were sunk. Strangely, the only survivor, the Hull trawler *Dromio*, was to sink some five days later after being run down by an Italian vessel north of Whitby.

Air attacks on trawlers became quite commonplace, and as a result many trawlers were armed with Lewis guns. One Scarborough vessel, the steam drifter *Silver Line*, engaged in an action with a German Heinkel, and gunner Tom Watkinson drove the raider off. The Heinkel was shot down in fact, but it seems that a British Spitfire had achieved this, though the crew of the *Silver Line* thought at the time that they had made the kill. Another steam trawler that fought back was the *Persian Empire*. Skipper Thomas Robson fired distress rockets at a German plane which was attacking him, and though he didn't harm the raider he caused it to drop bombs wide of the mark.

Earlier in the war, on 28 December 1939, an old hazard had already reappeared when the Grimsby trawler *Resercho* netted a mine while fishing in Bridlington Bay. The mate said later that as they hauled the net, an explosion occurred and a sheet of flame enveloped the ship. Steam pipes burst, hot ashes from the boiler fires shot in the air and fell about them, and tons of water crashed down on to the deck. Amazingly, all the nine crew escaped with their lives; they hung on until the water cascaded off the deck, and were then able to signal a passing steamer just before they abandoned the sinking trawler.

6.   Yesterday, Today
and Tomorrow

It had taken thousands of years to develop the sailing trawlers
that reached their peak in the 1880s, yet no sooner had the type
been perfected than it was made obsolete by the advent of paddle
trawlers and then screw-trawlers. As we have seen, the paddlers
enjoyed only a short spell of success, and were outdated in little
more than twenty years. Screw-steam trawlers proved to be more
successful; coal-burning steam-trawlers were in use for about half a
century, while oil-burning steam-trawlers are still in use today.
Coal proved to be such a bulky fuel that it took up a great deal of
space inside the ship, and besides this, oil was to prove a much
cheaper fuel too—though today, no form of fuel can be described
as cheap! As in most other walks of life, technology came to the
fishing industry about a hundred years ago; before that time progress
had been very slow. Surprisingly though, the actual methods of
catching the fish have changed very little, particularly for inshore
fishing.

Early in the twentieth century, a number of old sailing fishing
boats were fitted with internal-combustion petrol engines. One
of the earliest of these was the *Jane and Pricilla*, a 19 ton herring-
mule that had been built in 1880 and was owned by Arthur Douglas
of Filey. In 1907 this vessel had a petrol engine fitted, but on 15
September of the following year she sank off Robin Hood's Bay
with the loss of one man. Skipper Arthur Douglas was among the
survivors, and he had a new boat built which he called, appropriately, the *Thankful Arthur*. This boat too was fitted with a petrol
engine—an indication that Douglas was pleased with this new
form of propulsion.. Petrol engines had one big failing, however;
the spark-plugs and magnetos that they needed were very vulnerable
to water—and water was one thing in plentiful supply where the
fishermen worked! The diesel-engine of course solved this problem,
for it required neither of these electrical devices, and thus was
eminently suitable for marine use. A marine diesel engine can be
drenched in water, yet will continue to run, while such treatment
would stop a petrol engine in its tracks.

Among the bigger fishing craft there was some reluctance to adopt the use of diesel power as an alternative to steam-engines, and this was not simply due to natural conservatism. Fishermen needed power not only for propulsion, but also to drive the winches that hauled the nets. Steam-powered winches had proved themselves to be very reliable, and fishermen had come to put a lot of faith in them. The winch on a trawler is of course of paramount importance, and a failure on the part of the winch renders a fishing boat useless. However, these fears about losing the reliability of steam were gradually overcome, and the first diesel-powered trawler appeared in the early 1920s. Within ten years, many of Scarborough's inshore trawlers (or keelboats, as they are known locally) were equipped with diesel engines. Incidentally, the name "keelboat" dates back to the days of sailing vessels, and was used to distinguish a type of craft which had a keel from the the traditional coble which had no keel. For some reason the name stuck, and even today people refer to the fishing boats in Yorkshire's harbours as either cobles or keelboats

Just before World War II, deep-sea trawlers were being built with diesel-engines installed in them, but even as late as the 1950s some fishermen had their doubts about the advantages of these. The evolution of bigger and more powerful fishing vessels was not merely an exercise in technology, of course; it was necessary because fish were becoming harder to find. As has been mentioned earlier, by the 1880s the North Sea was being over-fished and trawlers had to go further afield in search of their catches. During World War I, few trawlers worked the North Sea grounds for obvious reasons and fish stocks were replenished naturally. However, when peace time returned in 1919 there were many bigger trawlers working here, and within twenty years the position regarding fish in the North Sea was worse than it had been in 1914. Since that time fish stocks have diminished year by year.

In the period since World War II, fishing vessel losses off the Yorkshire coast have declined dramatically, partly because there are fewer vessels working here, and partly because those that remain are so much more seaworthy. The introduction of electronic aids to navigation, better ships and better qualified skippers have all helped to reduce the casualty rate, but the dangers have not been completely eliminated by any means.

On 23 August 1959 the 472 ton Hull trawler *Staxton Wyke* became a victim of that age-old hazard, collision at sea. She was run down at 1-30 a.m. by the 11,000 ton ore carrier *Dalhanna* of Newcastle, some ten miles south of Flamborough Head. The *Staxton Wyke*, homeward bound through dense night-time fog, was so badly damaged that she sank in 90 seconds, taking five of her twenty-one crew with her. The sixteen survivors got into inflatable liferafts, and waited until the motor vessel *Dalhanna* came near them. Eventually they were taken aboard and a search was made for the five missing men, but none was found. Shortly after 4-00 a.m.

The herring fleet anchored off Scarborough. Pleasure steamer in the Bay is P.S. *Scarborough*

Paddle trawler *Fearless* reversing out of Scarborough harbour

The *Star* rescued the crew of another paddle trawler that sank in rough weather

Paddle trawler *Dunrobin* stranded at Seaton, where she became a total wreck

Giant waves pound the Icelandic trawler *Andri*, stranded at Kettleness on 25 January 1936. She was refloated later

Steam trawler *James Lay* of London, stranded on Filey Brigg, 13 January 1932, and refloated later

The bows of the steam trawler *Passing* after striking a mine in December 1914

Scarborough keelboat *Sincere* stranded south of Cayton Bay where she became a wreck, May 1968

the Flamborough lifeboat *Friendly Forester* arrived on the scene, and the lifeboat coxswain boarded the *Dalhanna* in order to speak to Andrew Whitely, skipper of the ill-fated trawler. The sixteen survivors were taken aboard the lifeboat, and the search was continued with the assistance of a passing steamship, the *Clarity*, and other vessels that were in the vicinity. Two empty rubber rafts were found, but still no trace of the missing men, and eventually hope was given up. The Flamborough lifeboat arrived back on station at 10-00a.m.

Another tragedy of this kind happened two years later on 18 October 1961, when heavy seas alone caused the loss of a large distant-water trawler. The 533 ton Hull trawler *Arctic Viking* was returning from a twenty-two day trip to the White Sea through a 50 m.p.h. gale. The seas were mountainous at the time, but this was no new experience for skipper Phil Garner or his eighteen crew. However, when the trawler was some twenty miles north-east of Flamborough Head, the ship was suddenly struck by an enormous wave which capsized her, and she sank quickly. Five men were drowned; fourteen others including the skipper were saved, being picked up by the Polish lugger *Derkacz*. The cause of the loss was thought to be a hatch which had not been battened down securely, thus allowing tons of water to enter when a sea swamped them. The *Arctic Viking* had had a dramatic career before this; built at Selby in 1937 as the *Arctic Pioneer*, she had been re-built at West Hartlepool ten years later. In May 1959, she had been involved in the first "Cod-War" when an Icelandic gunboat had fired twelve warning shots at her. This incident was brought to a close by the intervention of a Royal Navy ship.

These two events were of course well recorded by the press, but when smaller fishing boats were wrecked without loss of life it hardly warranted a mention. This is still true of today, an indication that we regard shipwreck as almost an accepted part of the fisherman's lot. A surprising number of inshore trawlers have in fact been lost off the Yorkshire coast within the last few years. Two keelboats were wrecked after stranding in fog during the early summer of 1968 and, because no lives were lost, few people even locally were aware of these losses. The Scarborough vessel *Sincere* ran aground on the southern side of Yons Nab, a promontory a few miles south of Scarborough, on 28 May where she became a total wreck. Her remains can be seen still, high and dry at low tide. A month later, on 30 June, the Whitby keelboat *Chrysolite* stranded and became a wreck on the north side of Filey Brigg. Built in Scotland in 1947, the *Chrysolite* had been working from Bridlington at the time of her loss.

On 28 November 1968 the Scarborough keelboat *Mary Joy* foundered off Whitby, and on 8 November 1971 the Bridlington keelboat *Welfare* stranded and became a total loss at Barmston, a

57

Steam drifter of 1925

few miles south of Bridlington. The most recent trawler wreck on the Yorkshire coast occurred on 2 April 1973, when the Grimsby vessel *White Knight* foundered after she ran ashore, following an engine failure. The five crew members were rescued by the crew of the Bridlington lifeboat in a force twelve gale and appalling sea conditions. For this gallant rescue Coxswain John King was awarded the R.N.L.I. Silver Medal; one of the only two such medals won in England in the year.

What of the future? It is difficult to see just where the future of the fishing industry lies, and so many forecasts in the past have proved wrong that it is perhaps wiser to wait and see! Things have changed to a great extent in some ways, yet have remained the same in others during the last hundred years. One interesting feature is the financial aspect of the industry, and the way in which costs have escalated over the past century. In 1880, a fully equipped, brand new sailing trawler could be bought for £1,500 or less. Steam trawlers a few years later cost in the region of £3,500 when new. Today, a 32 foot coble with gear can cost as much as £10,000, and an inshore trawler equipped with all the latest electronic aids costs almost £80,000. The trawlers that work in and around the Arctic Circle can today cost a staggering half-a-million pounds each. Little wonder then that the British fishing fleet brings back catches valued at over £150 million each year—they have to do to stay solvent!

As more and more nations become aware of the danger of overfishing, fishing limits are being extended, thus reducing

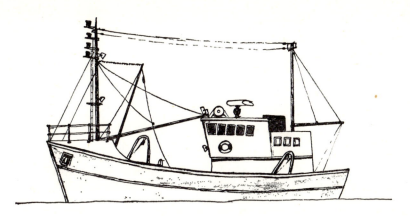

Inshore trawler of 1974

the areas left for our deep-sea fishermen to work in. As a result of this, they are looking to new and previously untapped sources for fish. In February 1974 the stern trawler *Luneda* made history when she became the first trawler to sell a catch of deep-water fish caught in the Atlantic. Previous visits had been made to these grounds on an experimental basis, but the *Luneda* was the first ship to sell a catch from this area. Though the response to the new kinds of fish was said to be encouraging, there is no doubt that many people looked at them with some apprehension. Instead of cod, haddock, plaice and skate, the *Luneda* brought back grenadiers, scabbard, mora, blue-ling and gephyroberyx, and faced a barrage of television cameras and newspaper reporters on her return. These fish had been caught at depths of between 200 and 700 fathoms, something that could not have been attempted until recently. Perhaps this is where the future of the industry lies—in the murky depths of the world's deep oceans.

Perhaps also the answer lies in fish-farming; this is not an entirely new idea, but so far no perfect method of accomplishing it has been found, and the costs are likely to be very high. In some areas of the world, attempts to increase fish stocks in coastal waters have been made by "fertilizing" the sea with phosphates and nitrogen. Methods of catching fish are almost certain to change too; present day freezer-trawlers are already a far cry from the trawlers of 50 years ago, and who knows what the trawlers of 50 years hence will be like? Perhaps they will not even be trawlers; the Russians have experimented with fishing-submarines already, and they have also used ships which attract fish by use of underwater lights and suck the catch out of the water with large suction-tubes.

And what of the fishermen themselves? In the "Ballad of Robin Hood" we read that:

> *The fishermen brave more money have*
> *Than any merchants two or three;*
> *Therefore I will to Scarborough go,*
> *That I a fisherman brave may be.*

Whether this reflected the true state of things in those far-off days is now a matter for speculation, but traditionally fishermen have not enjoyed a high standard of living. Many in fact have had to suffer extreme poverty on top of all the other hardships in their lives, and prolonged bad weather could until comparatively recently cause them and their families to go hungry. Today the position is much improved, and for the first time for many years fishermen can be said to be fairly well paid. Deep-sea trawler skippers are in fact very highly paid—and deservedly so—but their job security is worse than that of a casual labourer, for a skipper is in effect as good as his last trip in the eyes of his crew, his colleagues and the owners. Risk in every sense of the word, is the heritage of the fisherman today, as it always has been.

APPENDIX 1 : SAILING FISHING CRAFT LOSSES.

KEY : SH—Scarborough; GY—Grimsby; H—Hull; LT—Lowestoft; WY—Whitby; YH—Yarmouth; HL—Hartlepool; A—Aberdeen; LL—Liverpool; SD—Sunderland.

Name	Port	Date	Remarks	Page No.
ACHILLES	SH	3. 9.1898	Lost at sea	
ACTIVE	LL	6. 3.1883	Stranded near Spa, Scarborough	20
ADMIRAL HOPE	SH	28.10.1880	Stranded 1m N of Bridlington	18
ADVENTURE	GY	17. 8.1882	Collision 6m SE by S of Flamborough	
ALEXANDRA	SH	21. 5.1885	Lost at sea	
ALEXANDRA	SH	7. 1.1887	Foundered at sea	
ANDREW MARVEL	H	6. 3.1883	Lost in great gale	
ANN	WY	1882	Wrecked Filey Bay	
ANN	GY	14. 7.1868	Foundered off Flamborough Head	
ANN SIMS	H	6. 3.1883	Lost in great gale	
ATTRACTION	SH	6. 1.1865	Lost at sea	
BERNICE	H	6. 3.1883	Lost in great gale	
BESSIE LEWIS	H	6. 3.1883	Lost in great gale	
BLUE BELLE	GY	20.11.1880	Burnt near Silver Pits	
BRILLIANT	H	6. 3.1883	Lost in great gale	
BRITANNIA	H	6. 3.1883	Lost in great gale	
BRITANNIA		12.1857	Wrecked on Hornsea Beach	
BRITISH ROVER	SH	26.10.1859	Lost at sea	
BURTON STATHER	H	6. 3.1883	Lost in great gale	
CALEDONIA	A	27. 3.1808	Wrecked Salt Scar, Redcar	
CAPERNAUM	SH	14. 5.1894	Collision off Flamborough Head	
CECIL	GY	27.10.1897	Collision 20m E by N of Spurn	
CHARITY	SH	21.11.1860	Wrecked at Scarborough	
CHARITY	SH	21. 1.1872	Stranded Horse Rocks, N of Filey	
CHARLES & SARAH	SH	21.11.1862	Lost at sea	
CHARLES WESLEY	SH	28. 5.1860	Lost in hurricane	
CHOICE	SH	21. 5.1867	Lost at sea	

Name	Port	Date	Remarks	Page No.
CHOICE FLOWER	H	16.12.1893	Collision off Spurn	
CLARA	H	6. 3.1883	Lost in great gale	
CLARENCE	YH	6. 3.1883	Lost in great gale	
COLLECTOR	GY	27. 9.1875	Foundered on Dogger Bank	
CONCORD	SH	28. 5.1860	Lost in hurricane	
CORNELIA	GY	6. 3.1883	Lost in great gale	
CORNELIA	SH	6. 3.1883	Lost in great gale	19
CROWN	SH	29.12.1893	Collision off Flamborough	
CRUSOE	YH	17. 2.1871	Collision with smack *Teetotaler*	
DALTON LASS	HL	16. 6.1869	Stranded off Saltburn	
DART	H	6. 3.1883	Lost in great gale	
DEFENCE	GY	16.12.1882	Stranded near Spurn Point	
DENISON	SH	4. 8.1904	Foundered off Saltburn	
DILIGENCE	SH	25. 5.1860	Lost in hurricane	
DONCASTER	H	6. 3.1883	Lost in great gale	
DOVE	H	6. 3.1883	Lost in great gale	
ECONOMY	GY	14. 2.1870	Foundered on Dogger Bank	
EDITH	GY	17. 2.1881	Collision off Spurn	
EDITH	SH	6. 3.1883	Lost in great gale	
EFFORT	GY	4.1886	Stranded near Dimlington	
ELIZA	SH	22.12.1879	Lost at sea	
ELIZABETH & EMMA	SH	28.10.1880	Wrecked in Robin Hood's Bay	
ELIZABETH & SUSANNAH	SH	1. 2.1884	Wrecked on E pier, Scarboro'	
EMMA	GY	8.12.1882	Stranded near Whitby	
EMPRESS	SH	22.12.1879	Lost at sea	
EMU	GY	6. 3.1883	Lost in great gale	
EMULOUS	SH	24. 2.1884	Wrecked at Scarborough	
ENGLAND'S GLORY		29. 3.1879	Wrecked near Hayburn Wyke	
ENTERPRIZE	SH	12. 1.1884	Lost at sea	
EVELYN & MAUD	SH	16.11.1893	Lost at sea	
EXCELSIOR	GY	23. 1.1879	Stranded near Withernsea	
FAIR SUSAN	SH	1822	Lost at sea	
FAVOURITE	HL	1. 2.1884	Stranded near Scarborough	
FIBROUS	SH	1. 2.1868	Lost off Scarborough	
FIVE BROTHERS	SH	15.12.1898	Stranded near Scalby Mills	
FOUR GOOD BROTHERS	Dutch	28. 6.1881	Sank on Dogger Bank	
FOXHOUND	SH	13. 1.1881	Lost at sea	
FRIENDSHIP	YH	1.1823	Lost near Filey	
FRIEND'S GOOD WILL	H	6. 3.1883	Lost in great gale	
FRIEND'S INTEGRITY		1.1816	Sank on Dogger Bank	
GARIBALDI	SH	15.11.1878	Lost at sea	
GAUNTLET	SH	29.10.1880	Stranded Speeton Cliffs	18
GENERAL LEE	SH	28.10.1880	Lost at sea	18
GEORGE MOODY	GY	13. 2.1887	Sank off Spurn Point	
GEORGE PEABODY	SH	22.11.1888	Lost off Scarborough	
GRATITUDE	SH	2.12.1872	Collision off Scarborough	
HAPPY RETURN	WY	1822	Wrecked Filey Bay	
HARRIER	H	6. 3.1883	Lost in great gale	

Name	Port	Date	Remarks	Page No.
HARRY SINCLAIR	GY	16.11.1893	Stranded near Withernsea	
HESTER	SH	29. 4.1882	Lost near Whitby	
HOPE	SH	28. 5.1860	Lost in Filey Bay	
HOPE	SH	14.10.1874	Run down at sea	
HOPE	SH	28. 9.1875	Wrecked Port Mulgrave	
INO	SH	28. 5.1860	Wrecked Filey Bay	
INTEGRITY	SH	6. 3.1883	Lost off Filey in great gale	
INTREPID	SH	12.12.1883	Collision with *Queen of England*	
ISABELLE	HL	26.10.1880	Stranded at Redcar	
JAMES & ELLEN	SH	31.10.1897	Wrecked Horse Rocks, N of Filey	
JANE & MARY	LH	1.12.1897	Lost off Scarborough	
JANE & PRICILLA	SH	15. 9.1908	Sank off Whitby	51
JANE LANDER	St. Ives	3. 9.1902	Collision off Scarborough	
JEROME	SH	24. 2.1844	Wrecked at Scarborough	
JOHN & ELIZABETH	SH	26. 9.1851	Wrecked at Filey	
JOHN & ELIZABETH	SH	26.12.1855	Stranded at Speeton	
JOHN HARKER	H	6. 3.1883	Lost in great gale	
JOHN ROGERS	H	6. 3.1883	Lost in great gale	
JOHN WESLEY	SH	27.10.1880	Lost off Scarborough	17
KITTY	GY	17.12.1893	Sank off Spurn Point	
LARK	GY	6. 3.1883	Lost in great gale	
LEADER	GY	6. 3.1883	Lost in great gale	
LIBERTY	GY	1860	Stranded near Withernsea	
LILY	GY	6. 1.1881	Lost at sea	
LILY	H	6. 3.1883	Lost in great gale	
LINNET	LT	28. 9.1889	Wrecked S of Scarborough	
LIVELY	H	6. 3.1883	Lost in great gale	
LIZZIE GALE	H	6. 3.1883	Lost in great gale	
LOCH LONG	H	6. 3.1883	Lost in great gale	
LOUISE OF LORNE	H	13. 1.1881	Lost at sea	
MAID OF THE MILL	SH	11. 1.1887	Wrecked outer pier, Scarboro'	
MARGARET	LT	9. 9.1880	Stranded outer pier, Scarboro'	
MARY ANN GARDINER		4. 8.1855	Run down off Whitby	
MARY ANNS	SH	9.12.1874	Wrecked near Scarborough	
MARY ESTHER	H	6. 3.1883	Lost in great gale	
MASCOTTE	YH	6. 3.1883	Lost in great gale	
MASTERPIECE	H	20.10.1881	Lost at sea	
MAUDE & FLORENCE	SH	22. 2.1891	Wrecked at Whitby	
MOSQUITO	GY	6. 3.1883	Lost in great gale	
MYRTLE	GY	3. 2.1888	Run down off Spurn Point	
NEWARK	H	10. 3.1865	Sank near Dogger Bank	
NIL DESPERANDUM	SH	22.12.1894	Lost at sea	
NORFOLK LASS	SH	2.12.1862	Lost at sea	
NORTH SEA	H	6. 3.1883	Lost in great gale	
OCEAN	SH	4. 3.1877	Collision off Scarborough	
OLGA	GY	6. 3.1883	Lost in great gale	

Name	Port	Date	Remarks	Page No.
OLIVE	GY	26. 1.1865	Run down near Silver Pits	
OTTER	GY	6. 3.1883	Lost in great gale	
PALLAS	H	1.12.1893	Lost at sea	
PATRIOT	H	6. 3.1883	Lost in great gale	
PERSEVERANCE	SH	1828	Lost off Whitby	
PERSEVERANCE	SH	17.11.1865	Lost at sea	
POSTBOY	SH	16. 6.1854	Stranded at Scarborough	
PROGRESS	SH	25. 1.1876	Run down off Flamborough	
PROSPERITY	SH	27.10.1869	Lost off Scarborough	17
PROSPEROUS	Rams-gate	9.12.1854	Stranded near Scarborough Spa	
PROVIDENCE	SH	3. 1.1839	Lost off Whitby	
QUEEN OF ENGLAND	SH	12.12.1883	Collision with *Intrepid*	
RAMBLER	SH	27.10.1869	Lost at sea	17
REAPER	SH	8. 3.1845	Run down off Flamborough	
REAPER	YH	6. 3.1883	Lost in great gale	
RELIANCE	GY	21. 3.1879	Stranded near Spurn	
RIPPLING WAVE	GY	5. 1.1894	Collision at sea	
RISING SUN	SH	2.11.1861	Lost at sea	
RISING SUN		10. 1.1883	Stranded at Dimlington	
RIVER KING		30. 1.1870	Collision off Scarborough	
ROBERT NEWTON	SH	28. 5.1860	Wrecked Filey Bay	
ROSE	H	6. 3.1883	Lost in great gale	
ROSE OF KENT	GY	7. 7.1865	Sank off Scarborough	
RUBY	SH	14.10.1881	Lost off Scarborough	
ST. PAUL	WY	2.10.1880	Sank off Whitby	
SCARBOROUGH KING	SH	12.11.1879	Lost at sea	
SCEPTRE	H	13. 1.1881	Lost at sea	
SEA DRIFT	SH	28.12.1886	Wrecked at Staithes	
SEA FLOWER	YH	6. 3.1883	Lost in great gale	
SECRET	GY	5.10.1880	Stranded at Filey	
SISTERS	SH	12. 3.1875	Collision off Flamborough	
SOVEREIGN	H	3.12.1867	Sank off Humber	
SPIRIT OF THE AGE	SH	6. 1.1865	Lost at sea	
SPRAY	SH	28.10.1880	Wrecked near Bridlington	18
SPY	SH	18. 4.1899	Wrecked at Speeton	
SUNBEAM	H	6. 3.1883	Lost in great gale	
SYLVIA	GY	15.10.1895	Wrecked in Cayton Bay	
TEAZER	SH	28. 3.1878	Wrecked at Scarborough	
TEETOTALER	Rams-gate	17. 2.1871	Collision with smack *Crusoe*	
THE BOYS	H	6. 3.1883	Lost in great gale	
THE POLLIES	SH	30. 1.1887	Lost at sea	
THOMAS & MARGARET	SH	2. 3.1881	Lost at sea	
THOMAS & MARY	SH	9. 3.1899	Lost at sea	
THOMAS & WILLIAM	SH	2. 6.1882	Stranded N of Scarborough	
THREE BROTHERS	SH	28. 5.1860	Lost at Filey	
TOILERS OF THE SEA	SH	11. 1.1899	Lost at sea	
TRIO	SH	14. 5.1895	Lost off Flamborough	
TURQUOISE		8.1890	Run down off Dogger Bank	

Name	Port	Date	Remarks	Page No.
TWO BROTHERS	GY	12. 5.1902	Wrecked off Spurn	
TWO FRIENDS	SH	1847	Wrecked at Scarborough	
UNEXPECTED		1. 9.1853	Stranded at Scarborough	
UNITY	SH	28. 4.1892	Lost off Filey	
UNO	H	6. 3.1883	Lost in great gale	
VAARWELL	Dutch	21. 3.1868	Collision near Dogger Bank	
VANGUARD	H	6. 3.1883	Lost in great gale	
VICTOR	SH	20. 1.1877	Lost at sea	
WANDERER	SH	9. 3.1882	Lost at sea	
WILLIAM & RICHARD	Rams-gate	16. 1.1852	Stranded near Withernsea	
WILLIAM GILLS	GY	6. 3.1883	Lost in great gale	
WILLING MIND	SH	18. 4.1822	Wrecked at Filey	
X.L.	SH	28. 3.1867	Run down off Scarborough	
YORKSHIRE LASS	H	25.12.1858	Wrecked at Scarborough	
YORKSHIRE LASS	WY	3. 5.1881	Sank near Whitby harbour	
YOUNG ALFRED	SH	12.12.1881	Run down at sea	
YOUNG ALICE	SH	16. 3.1890	Wrecked off Scarborough	
ZILLAH & RACHEL	SH	28. 5.1860	Wrecked in Filey Bay	
ZIPPORAH	SH	30. 8.1881	Lost off Runswick Bay	

APPENDIX 2 STEAM FISHING BOAT LOSSES

Name	Port	Date	Remarks	Page No.
ADVENTURE	H	20. 2.1889	Foundered near Dogger Bank	
AKRANES	GY	4. 7.1941	Sunk by aircraft near South Landing	
ALBATROSS	GY	24. 9.1916	Sunk by U-boat 20m E of Flamborough	
ALPHA	Shields	7.10.1889	Run down 15m ENE of Spurn	26
APHELION	GY	25. 9.1916	Sunk by U-boat 20m E of Flamborough	
ARCTIC	GY	20. 1.1909	Collision 5m E by N of Flamborough	
ARNDILLY CASTLE		25.11.1925	Sank in Bridlington Bay in storm	
AUCUBA	GY	5. 9.1951	Collision off Robin Hood's Bay	41
BAHRAM	GY	3. 4.1941	Mined in Humbermouth	
BALTIC	GY	29. 2.1916	Stranded Bempton Cliffs	
BANYERS	GY	6. 1.1915	Mined off Scarborough	43
BENGAL		18.12.1929	Stranded near Withernsea	
BRITISH EMPIRE	H	27. 2.1900	Stranded Bempton Cliffs	
BRITON	GY	25. 9.1916	Sunk by U-boat 20m E of Flamborough	

Name	Port	Date	Remarks	Page No.
BUCKINGHAM	GY	10.12.1904	Stranded near Withernsea	
BUSTARD	GY	13.10.1908	Collision off Whitby	
CAPRICORNUS	GY	22. 8.1914	Sunk by torpedo boat off Spurn	
CARDIFF	GY	9. 6.1915	Sunk by U-boat off Whitby	
CARLTON	GY	25.10.1940	Mined 3½m off Spurn	
CASORIA	GY	26. 2.1920	Mined 25m ENE of Flamborough	49
CASTOR	GY	9. 6.1915	Sunk by U-boat off Whitby	
CHEVY CHASE	SD	6.10.1886	Stranded Horse Rocks, N of Filey	26
CHILIAN	GY	9. 4.1894	Stranded on Filey Brigg	32
CONDOR	SH	29. 5.1915	Mined NE of Scarborough	44
COURTIER	GY	6. 1.1916	Mined off Kilnsea	
CRAWFORD		27.11.1910	Ashore S of Flamborough	
CRUX	GY	10. 1.1912	Stranded S of Withernsea	
CRYSTAL	H	26. 6.1943	Mined off Scarborough	
CYNTHIA	GY	24. 9.1916	Sunk by U-boat off Flamborough	
CYRANO	GY	4. 3.1905	Run down 130m NE by N of Spurn	
DALHOUSIE	SH	13. 7.1916	Sunk by U-boat 10m NNE of Whitby	44
DEVONIAN	GY	8. 9.1915	Mined 30m NE by N of Spurn	
DEVONSHIRE	GY	24. 9.1916	Sunk by U-boat off Flamborough	
DIAMOND	H	9. 1.1912	Stranded at Speeton	
DINORAH	A	28. 4.1945	Mined off Bridlington	
DIRK		28. 5.1918	Sunk off Flamborough	
DORIC	GY	14.12.1899	Stranded Kettleness Point	
DROMIO	H	22.12.1939	Collision off Whitby	50
EMULATOR	SH	15. 4.1919	Mined 26m off Flamborough	49
ETRURIA	H	15.12.1903	Stranded 7m N of Scarborough	37
EUROPE	GY	7. 1.1910	Run down 30m NE of Spurn	
EUTHAMIA	GY	22. 9.1918	Mined off Spurn	
EVENING STAR	SH	12. 8.1908	Sunk 35m off Scarborough	
FALMOUTH	GY	12. 4.1945	Mined off Humbermouth	
FEARLESS	SH	30. 4.1901	Stranded Blea Wyke, Robin Hood's Bay	28
FERMO	GY	10.11.1917	Collision 3m NE of Spurn	
FISHER PRINCE	SH	25. 9.1916	Sunk by U-boat 20m NE of Scarborough	
FLORENCE	SH	13. 7.1916	Sunk by U-boat 10m NE of Scarborough	44
GAMECOCK	SH	25. 9.1916	Sunk by U-boat 20m NE of Scarborough	
GARMO	GY	20.12.1914	Mined off Scarborough	43
GOLDEN GLEAM	GY	10.10.1917	Run down off Whitby	
GOLDEN SCEPTRE	H	16. 1.1912	Stranded Kettleness	
GREENOCK	GY	12.11.1915	Foundered 85m E by N of Spurn	
GRIMBARIAN	GY	4. 8.1915	Mined 56m E by N of Spurn	

Name	Port	Date	Remarks	Page No.
HAINTON	GY	11. 7.1915	Sunk by U-boat 45m NE by N of Spurn	
HARRIER	SH	25. 9.1916	Sunk by U-boat 20m NE of Scarborough	
JACK JOHNSON	SH	3. 9.1920	Mined 48m E by S of Tyne	49
JENNIE BULLAS	GY	4.10.1916	Sunk by U-boat 14m ENE of Spurn	
JERSEY	GY	4.10.1916	Sunk by U-boat 16m NE by N of Spurn	
JOSEPH BURGIN	GY	16.11.1933	Foundered 75m ENE of Spurn	
KERNOOZER	H	19. 3.1943	Wrecked at Skipsea	
KIMBERLEY	GY	29. 3.1941	Sunk by aircraft in Bridlington Bay	
KING CHARLES	GY	17. 5.1915	Sunk by torpedo boat, Dogger Bank	
LACONIA	GY	17. 5.1911	Collision 3m ENE of Flamborough	
LAPWING	GY	6. 6.1940	Mined off Barmston	
LARK	H	13.12.1911	Stranded at Bempton	
LAUREL	GY	23. 1.1920	Collision 28m NE of Spurn	
LINDUM	GY	6.10.1916	Stranded North Landing, Flamborough	
LISMORE	GY	11. 5.1907	Collision 20m NE of Spurn	
LOCHIEL		24. 7.1918	Sunk off Saltburn	
LOCH NESS		25. 9.1916	Sunk by U-boat 20m NE of Scarborough	
LONICERA	Banff	28. 9.1933	Stranded Casty Rocks, Gristhorpe	
LORD AIREDALE	GY	18. 3.1915	Stranded Bridlington, refloated later	49
LORD CLYDE	SH	12.12.1893	Run down off Scarborough	27
LORD ERNLE	GY	4. 3.1937	Stranded Staple Nook, Bempton	39
LORD RIDLEY	GY	10. 5.1917	Mined off Whitby	
LUCERNE	GY	21.10.1931	Collision near Spurn Lightship	
MAGNETA	H	24. 1.1908	Stranded near Hayburn Wyke	
MAJESTIC	GY	10. 1.1917	Stranded Robin Hood's Bay	
MANX QUEEN	GY	1. 3.1916	Stranded Filey Brigg	
MARGATE	GY	24. 4.1917	Sunk by U-boat off Spurn	
MARGUERITE	SH	25. 9.1916	Sunk by U-boat 20m NE of Scarborough	
MARIE JOSEPH		11.11.1891	Sank NE of Scarborough	26
MATABELE	H	18.12.1938	Wrecked near Teesmouth	
MAYBIRD	HL	6. 3.1883	Stranded at Scarborough	20
MAYFLY	GY	24. 4.1917	Sunk by U-boat off Flamborough	
MEDIATOR	A	2. 1.1916	Mined off Hornsea	
MEG		5. 6.1936	Stranded Scalby, near Scarborough	
MERRIE ISLINGTON	H	6. 5.1915	Sunk by U-boat 6m off Whitby	44
MIDGE	H	27. 1.1896	Stranded at Speeton	

Name	Port	Date	Remarks	Page No.
NATION'S HOPE	Shields	28.10.1880	Foundered off Port Mulgrave	26
NERO		21.12.1904	(Norwegian) Stranded near Flamborough	
NIGHTHAWK	GY	25.12.1914	Mined off Scarborough	43
NIL DESPERANDUM	SH	25. 9.1916	Sunk by U-boat 20m NE of Scarborough	
NORDRIFT	GY	30.10.1937	Stranded Easington	
NORENDA		1922	Sank off Burniston, Scarborough	
NOTTINGHAM	GY	7. 6.1915	Sunk by U-boat 70m NE of Spurn	
OPHIR II	GY	7. 9.1941	Mined 15m off Spurn	
ORIANDA	GY	19.12.1914	Mined off Cayton Bay, Scarborough	43
ORION	GY	15. 6.1906	Foundered 60m NE of Spurn	
OTTER	SH	25. 9.1916	Sunk by U-boat 20m NE of Scarborough	31, 37
OTTERHOUND	SH	25. 9.1916	Sunk by U-boat 20m NE of Scarborough	
PELICAN	H	30.12.1909	Stranded N of Flamborough Head	
PICADOR	H	4.1936	Collision off Flamborough	
PLYMOUTH	GY	11. 6.1915	Sunk by U-boat off Flamborough	
POINTER	H	3.12.1904	Stranded Flamborough Head	
PREMIER	GY	10. 2.1923	Stranded 3m S of Robin Hood's Bay	
PRIME MINISTER	H	18. 9.1903	Stranded near Peak, Ravenscar	37
PROFICIENT	LT	19.12.1940	Stranded at Whitby	
QUEBEC	SH	25. 9.1916	Sunk by U-boat 20m NE of Scarborough	
RADO	GY	4.10.1916	Sunk by U-boat 15m NE by N of Spurn	
REBONO	GY	23. 9.1914	Mined 25m E by N of Spurn	
RECEPTO	GY	16. 2.1917	Sunk near Teesmouth	
RECOLO	GY	26. 4.1915	Mined 60m E by N of Spurn	
REPERIO		28.12.1908	Stranded Robin Hood's Bay	
RESEARCH	H	25.11.1925	Sank on Smethwick Sands, Bridlington	40
RESERCHO	GY	28.12.1939	Mined off Bridlington	50
REVIGO	GY	7. 9.1914	Mined 25m off Spurn	
REX	GY	8.10.1903	Collision near Spurn	
RHODESIA	GY	18.12.1916	Foundered 60m ENE of Flamborough	
RIVER DON	GY	27.10.1931	Foundered 7m N of Spurn	
RIVIERE	GY	10. 6.1953	Collision 5m off Flamborough	
ROCHESTER	LT	27. 7.1944	Mined off Hornsea	
ROMAN EMPIRE	H	14.12.1923	Foundered 40m ENE of Flamborough	
ROSELLA	GY	5.11.1914	Mined off Teesmouth	
ROYALLIEU	H	6. 4.1906	Stranded at Bempton	
RUBICO	GY	9. 3.1904	Collision 45m NNE of Spurn	

Name	Port	Date	Remarks	Page No.
WAAGO	GY	11. 6.1915	Sunk by U-boat off Flam-borough	
WALLSEND		25. 8.1903	Sank off Teesmouth	
WILLIAM TENNANT		5. 3.1918	Collision off Humber	
WINDSOR	GY	25.10.1940	Mined 2m off Spurn	
ZARINA	GY	7. 4.1915	Sunk by U-boat 72m E by N of Spurn	

APPENDIX 3 MOTOR FISHING VESSEL LOSSES

Name	Port	Date	Remarks	Page No.
ABY	GY	7. 7.1918	Sunk by U-boat 25m off Spurn	
ALBATROSS	SH	17.11.1940	Lost in Bridlington Bay, presumed mined.	
ALBION	GY	7. 7.1918	Sunk by U-boat 25m off Spurn	
ARROW		15.11.1923	Sank in Bridlington harbour-mouth	
BOTHA	SH	28. 3.1918	Sunk by U-boat 3m E of Whitby	
BROTHERLY LOVE	GY	28. 3.1918	Sunk by U-boat 6m NE by E of Whitby	
CHAUCER	GY	17.12.1919	Stranded Spurn Point	
CHRYSOLITE		30. 6.1968	Stranded on Filey Brigg	57
DUNTROON CASTLE	H	1. 8.1967	Foundered off Bridlington	
EDITH CAVELL	SH	5. 5.1917	Sunk by U-boat off Flamborough	44
GLEANER		5. 2.1909	Wrecked North Landing, Flamborough	
GLORIA		12.11.1927	Wrecked in Filey Bay	
GUIDING STAR		27. 1.1935	Sank in storm off Bridlington	
HONORA	WY	28. 3.1918S	Sunk by U-boat 6m ENE of Whitby	
LILY OF THE VALLEY		13. 7.1923	Caught fire, sank off Bridlington	
MARY JOY	SH	28.11.1968	Foundered off Whitby	57
MAY LILY		13. 1.1953	Foundered off Filey	
MEG		5. 6.1936	Stranded N of Scalby Mills, Scarborough	
NOEL	GY	6. 3.1918	Sunk by U-boat 6m NE by E of Whitby	
PRIDE	GY	16.10.1940	Mined off harbour, Scar-borough	

Name	Port	Date	Remarks	Page No.
PROTECT ME II	SH	17. 5.1935	Foundered 8m S of Bridlington	
QUEEN BEE	LT	4. 7.1916	Sunk by U-boat 28m NE of Scarborough	
ROSE OF JUNE	GY	28. 6.1917	Sunk by U-boat 10m NE of Spurn	
SINCERE		28. 5.1968	Stranded Yons Nab, S of Scarborough	57
SUSIE		17. 8.1917	Sunk by U-boat 10m NE of Scarborough	
TWO BROTHERS		5. 2.1909	Wrecked North Landing, Flamborough	
WELFARE		8.11.1971	Stranded near Barmston, Bridlington	57
WHINNYFOLD	GY	3. 2.1958	Stranded near Redcar	
WHITE KNIGHT		2. 4.1973	Abandoned off Easington	58
WILLIAM & BETSY	GY	28. 6.1917	Sunk 10m NE of Spurn	

BIBLIOGRAPHY AND ACKNOWLEDGEMENTS

The Yorkshire Coast, J. Leyland (London, 1892).

The Yorkshire Coast, B. Farnill (Dalesman, 1968).

Shipwrecks of the Yorkshire Coast, A. Godfrey & P. J. Lassey (Dalesman, 1974).

Yorkshire Ports and Harbours, B. F. Duckham (Dalesman, 1967).

Filey and its Fishermen, G. Shaw.

Sailing Trawlers, E. March (reprinted David & Charles).

Sailing Drifters, E. March (reprinted David & Charles).

The Sea-Fisheries of Great Britain & Ireland, G. L. Alward (1932).

British Fisheries, Johnstone (1905).

Inshore Craft of Britain in the days of Sail and Oar, (2 vols), E. March, (1970).

The Sea Fishing Industry of Eng.and & Wales, F. G. Aflalo (1904).

North Sea Fishers and Fighters, W. Wood (1911).

The Silver Haul, A. Jenkins (1967).

Fishermen at War, L. Walmsley (1941).

Spunyarn, Lt. H. B. Boothby (G. T. Foulis & Co.).

Loss List of Grimsby Vessels, D. Boswell (1969).

Deep Sea Fishing and Fishing Boats, E. W. Holdsworth (1874).

Vanishing Craft, F. G. Carr & F. Mason (London 1934).

I would like to thank the hundreds of people who have shared my interest and have helped to gather the information in this book. Particular thanks are due to the following, who have been especially helpful:

George Scales; Capt. S. Smith (retd.); George Westwood; David Whitaker; Arthur Wray; Peter Lassey; William Cappleman; and the staff at Scarborough Public Library.

The photographs on the pages listed below (T—top; B—bottom) were supplied as follows:-

Author's collection: 34B. 35T. 53T, 55B.

Doran Bros., Whitby: 55T.

G. Scales: 56B, back cover—B.

Scarborough Museums: 35B, 36, 56T.

Scarborough Public Library: 33 34T, 53B, 54, back cover—T.